P9-DCS-825

THE WONDERS OF SCIENCE

THE HUMAN BODY

Joan S. Gottlieb

STECK-VAUGHN
C O M P A N Y
A Subsidiary of National Education Corporation

ISBN 0-8114-4135-0
Copyright © 1990 Steck-Vaughn Company.
All rights reserved. No part of the material protected by this copyright
may be reproduced or utilized in any form or by any means, electronic
or mechanical, including photocopying, recording, or by any
information storage and retrieval system, without permission in
writing from the copyright owner. Requests for permission to make
copies of any part of the work should be mailed to:
Copyright Permissions, Steck-Vaughn Company, P.O. Box 26015,
Austin, TX 78755. Printed in the United States of America.

6 7 8 9 0 DBH 94 93 92

TABLE OF CONTENTS

UNIT 1 How the Body Is Organized

UNIT 2 Body Systems

UNIT 3 More Body Systems

UNIT 4 The Nervous System

What Is Human Biology?

You probably have questions about how your body works.

Why is exercise good for me?

What foods are best to eat?

Why do I get colds or the flu?
You will find the answers to many questions like these in this book.

This book is about human **biology.** Biology is the study of living things. And human biology tells you about your body.

Your body has a very important job. It is the job of living. To do its job, your body has many parts that work together.

Your heart pumps blood. Blood carries important materials to all parts of your body. Some of these materials come from food. Food gives your body the energy it needs to work.

Your body has bones that give it shape. Muscles are attached to bones. You move because muscles pull on your bones.

Your body has five senses. Senses let you know what is going on around you. The five senses are sight, hearing, taste, touch, and smell.

Your body is always working. Your heart keeps pumping even while you sleep. You also breathe in and out all the time. These jobs, and many others, are controlled by your brain. Your brain helps you think. It helps control your feelings.

You can see how important it is for all of the parts of your body to work together. Learn more about your body. Learn how to keep it working well.

A. Answer True or False.

1. In human biology, you learn about your body. _____

2. Bones give your body shape. _____

3. Muscles move bones. _____

4. You have five senses. _____

5. The brain pumps blood through the body. _____

B. Fill in the missing words.

1. You get the energy you need from _____. (bones, food)

2. Your _____ help you to move. (muscles, blood)

3. The _____ pumps blood through the body. (brain, heart)

4. When you think, you are using your _____. (brain, heart)

5. Sight is one of your five _____. (hearts, senses)

C. Underline the answer to each question.

1. What moves your arms and legs? (muscles, blood)

2. What helps you think and feel? (brain, bones)

3. What lets you know what is going on around you? (bones, senses)

4. What carries materials through the body? (muscles, blood)

5. What pumps blood through the body? (brain, heart)

D. Answer the questions.

1. When is your body working? _____

_____

2. How is your body like a car? _____

_____

3. Why is the brain an important part of your body? _____

_____

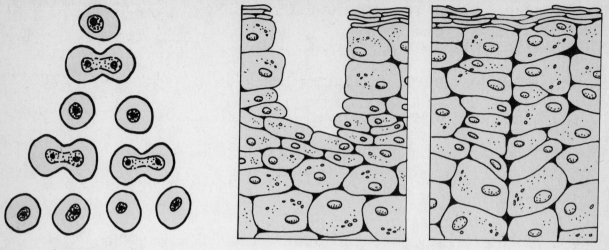

Cells Dividing

New cells heal a cut in the skin.

Look at the period at the end of this sentence. You may be surprised to learn that your body is made of parts that are smaller than that period!

Your body is made of **cells.** All living things are made of cells. Most cells are too small to see with your eyes alone. You have to use a tool called a **microscope.**

The cells of your body are like tiny factories. Each cell takes in food. Each cell gives off wastes. To live, a cell must do these jobs.

Cells can also grow and divide. When a cell divides, 1 cell becomes 2 cells. Then 2 cells become 4 cells. Dividing cells make you grow. Bone cells divide and make bones grow. Muscle cells divide and make muscles grow.

But even after you stop growing, your cells keep dividing. You can see this with skin cells. Suppose you fall and cut the skin on your knee. Your skin cells divide and make more cells. In about a week, new cells have filled in the cut.

Your body has millions and millions of cells. No one knows exactly how many. These cells have many different jobs. Bone cells do a special job. Blood cells do another job. But all the cells of your body work together. Together they do the job of living.

A. Fill in the missing words.

1. The smallest part of your body is _____. (a cell, your hand)

2. Your leg is made up of _____. (one cell, many cells)

3. All _____ are made of cells. (objects, living things)

4. When one cell divides, it makes _____ cells. (2, 4)

5. Cells take in _____. (food, wastes)

6. Cells give off _____. (food, wastes)

B. Answer True or False.

1. Cells are in all living things. _____

2. A plastic comb is made of cells. _____

3. You need a microscope to see some cells. _____

4. Cells divide and make more cells. _____

5. You grow because your cells divide. _____

6. When you stop growing, your cells stop dividing. _____

7. You are made up of one very large cell. _____

C. Answer the questions.

1. What are your body and all other living things made of? _____

_____

2. How do cells grow in number? _____

3. Most cells are very small. How could you see these cells? _____

_____

4. Name two jobs of a cell. _____

_____

5. Name three things that are made of cells. _____

_____

7

The Parts of a Cell

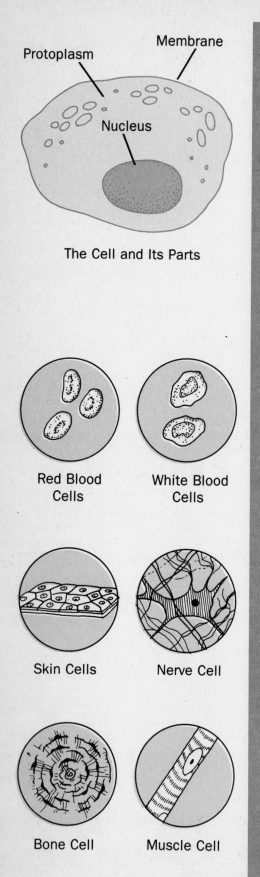

The Cell and Its Parts

Red Blood Cells

White Blood Cells

Skin Cells

Nerve Cell

Bone Cell

Muscle Cell

You know that cells are very small. Yet even tiny cells have different parts. Most cells have a **membrane.** The membrane is like your skin. When you sweat, wastes pass out of your skin. Wastes also pass out of the cell. They move out through the cell membrane. Food can move into the cell through the cell membrane.

Cells are filled with **protoplasm.** Protoplasm is a clear jelly. It holds many other small cell parts. Some of these parts store food and do other special jobs for the cell.

Most cells have a **nucleus.** The nucleus is like a tiny brain. The nucleus gives instructions to the cell. It tells a cell what kind it will be. It tells a cell what its job is in the body. The only cell in the body that does not have a nucleus is a red blood cell.

Some cells do special jobs. The way a cell looks is often a clue to the kind of work it does. **Fat cells** store large amounts of fat in the protoplasm. **Nerve cells** carry messages through the body. They have long parts that stretch out. These long parts are like telephone wires, carrying messages from one part of the body to another. **Skin cells** are flat. They protect the parts of the body that they cover.

Look at the first picture. It is a drawing of the different parts of a cell. The other pictures show you what different body cells look like through a microscope. Do all the cells look exactly alike?

A. Draw lines between the cell part and the job it does.

1. Protoplasm   tells the cell what its job is.

2. Nucleus   lets food and wastes in and out of the cell.

3. Membrane   holds small parts of the cell.

B. Label the parts of a cell.

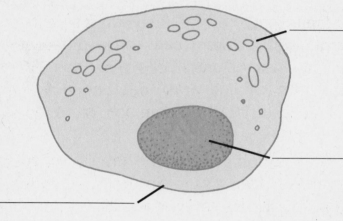

C. Complete each sentence. Use the words below.

membrane	nucleus	protoplasm

1. The part of the cell that acts like your skin is the _____.

2. The _____ gives instructions to the cell.

3. The clear jelly inside a cell is called _____.

4. Wastes can pass out of the cell through the _____.

D. Answer True or False.

1. All cells are the same. _____

2. Nerve cells carry messages. _____

3. Skin cells protect the parts of the body they cover. _____

4. Materials can move in and out of the cell membrane. _____

5. The nucleus tells a cell what its job is in the body. _____

Tissues

Muscle Tissue

Nerve Tissue

Bone Tissue

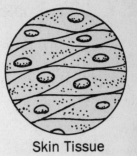
Skin Tissue

You know that cells are the smallest part of your body. And you know that different cells have different jobs. But cells do not work alone. Cells that look alike and that do the same job work together in a group. A group of cells doing the same job is called a **tissue.**

A group of skin cells doing the same job is called skin tissue. One kind of skin tissue covers your body. Another kind of skin tissue lines your mouth, stomach, and other body parts.

Your body has other kinds of tissues. Bundles of muscle cells form muscle tissue. You also have blood tissue, nerve tissue, and bone tissue.

A. Fill in the missing words.

1. Cells _____ work alone. (do, do not)

2. The smallest part of your body is a _____ . (cell, tissue)

3. A tissue is made up of _____ . (bones, cells)

4. Your body is covered by _____ tissue. (skin, muscle)

B. Answer the questions.

1. What is a tissue? _____

2. What is a group of nerve cells called? _____

3. Name three kinds of body tissue. _____

_____

Organs

What is happening as you read this page? Your heart is pumping. You breathe in and out with your lungs. Your eyes see the words on the page. Your brain helps you understand the words. All these body parts are examples of **organs.** An organ is a group of different tissues working together to do a job.

Your heart is made of blood tissue, nerve tissue, and muscle tissue. What is the job of your heart? Your skin has many different layers. Each layer has a different job. All the parts of your skin put together form an organ. Your stomach is an organ, too. Your stomach is an organ that helps in the job of breaking down food.

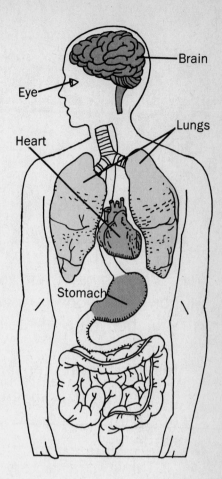

Brain

Eye

Lungs

Heart

Stomach

A. **Answer True or False.**

1. An organ is a group of tissues working together. _____

2. Your heart is a tissue. _____

3. Your eyes are organs. _____

4. A cell is larger than an organ. _____

B. **Fill in the missing words.**

1. The smallest part of your body is a _____. (cell, tissue)

2. Cells work together in groups called _____. (organs, tissues)

3. A group of tissues working together is called _____. (an organ, a tissue)

4. Your lungs are examples of _____. (cells, organs)

Systems

Your body systems are like parts of a factory.

Remember what you have learned so far about how your body is organized. The smallest parts of your body are its cells. A group of cells doing the same job forms a tissue. A group of tissues working together forms an organ.

Organs work in groups, too. A group of organs doing the same job is called a **system.** Your body is made up of many systems.

Think of a factory where cars are made. One part of the factory makes the metal body. Another part makes the tires. Still another part makes the glass. You must have all the parts to make a complete car.

Your body systems are like the parts of a factory. Each system does a different job. But the systems work together to keep you healthy.

A. Number these parts in order of size. Number 1 is the smallest part.

Tissue _____   Cell _____

Organ _____   System _____

B. Answer the question.

What do you think might happen if one of a person's body systems was

not working? _____

_____

Review

Part A

Fill in the missing word in each sentence. Use the words below.

biology	nucleus	system
cell	organ	tissue
membrane	protoplasm	

1. The study of living things is called _____.

2. The _____ is the smallest part of your body.

3. A group of cells forms a _____.

4. Your heart is an example of an _____.

5. The _____ gives instructions to the cell.

Part B

Label the parts of a cell. Use the words from the box above.

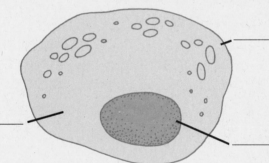

Part C

Answer the questions.

1. Name two jobs that cells do. _____

_____

2. What is a group of organs doing the same job called? _____

_____

3. Why is every system of your body important? _____

_____

Fill in the circle in front of the word or phrase that best completes the sentence. The first one is done for you.

1. In human biology, you learn about
   ● your body.
   ⓑ plants.
   ⓒ animals.

2. All living things are made of
   ⓐ plants.
   ⓑ animals.
   ⓒ cells.

3. To see very small cells, you can use
   ⓐ a camera.
   ⓑ your eyes.
   ⓒ a microscope.

4. Cells grow in number by
   ⓐ dividing.
   ⓑ getting bigger.
   ⓒ getting smaller.

5. Food goes into a cell through the
   ⓐ nucleus.
   ⓑ membrane.
   ⓒ organ.

6. The part that tells a cell its job is the
   ⓐ tissue.
   ⓑ nucleus.
   ⓒ membrane.

7. A group of cells doing the same job is called
   ⓐ a tissue.
   ⓑ an organ.
   ⓒ a system.

8. Your body is covered with
   ⓐ muscle tissue.
   ⓑ bone tissue.
   ⓒ skin tissue.

9. Your heart is an example of
   ⓐ a cell.
   ⓑ an organ.
   ⓒ a tissue.

10. A group of organs doing the same job is called
    ⓐ a system.
    ⓑ a tissue.
    ⓒ an organ.

Just for Fun

Each sentence below is about human biology. But one word in each sentence is scrambled. Unscramble the letters. Then write the correct word on the lines at the right. Choose from the words below. The first one is done for you.

biology	heart	nerve
body	human	organs
cells	muscles	tissue

1. LOGIOBY is the study of living things.

   B I O L O G Y
                9

2. NAMUH biology tells you about your body.

   _ _ _ _ _
   8

3. The cell is the smallest part of the DOBY.

   _ _ _ _
   1

4. A bundle of muscle cells forms a SITSUE.

   _ _ _ _ _ _
   7

5. The REATH is an organ.

   _ _ _ _ _
   3

6. A VERNE cell carries messages.

   _ _ _ _ _
     2   4

7. SCUMLES move bones.

   _ _ _ _ _ _ _
             6

8. Your eyes are GANORS of sight.

   _ _ _ _ _ _
         5

Solve the Secret Message. When a letter of a word above has a number under it, write that letter above the same number in the Secret Message.

Secret Message: If you know about your body, you can learn to

_ _ _ _ _ _ _ _ _
1 2 3 4 5 6 7 8 9

The Skeletal System

The Skeleton

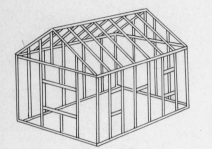

House Framework

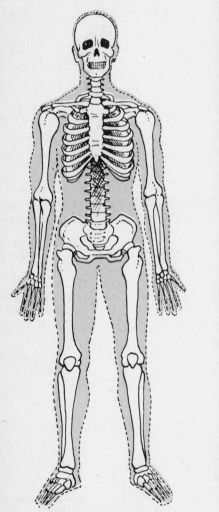

Body Framework

The framework of a house holds all the parts of the house in place. It gives the house its shape. You have a framework of bones called a **skeleton.** Your skeleton supports your body. It gives shape to your body. Without a skeleton you would not be able to stand up.

Your skeleton is made up of 206 bones of different shapes and sizes. There are tiny bones in your fingers, and long bones in your arms and legs. All the bones are part of your **skeletal system.** The bones of the skeletal system work together with muscles to produce movement. People can walk, run, wave their arms, and jump. All these motions and others are possible because muscles move the bones of the skeleton.

The bones of the skeleton also protect the soft parts of your body. Your heart and lungs are protected by a cage of rib bones. Your brain is covered by a bony skull. You will learn more about these bones as you read the rest of the unit.

Bones help the body in another way. The bones of the skeleton store minerals that the body needs. These minerals help keep the bones and teeth strong. Bones also make cells for the blood.

A. **Answer True or False.**

1. The skeleton gives your body shape. _____

2. A skeleton helps support your body. _____

16

3. The bones of the skeleton store important minerals. _____

4. Bones can move without muscles. _____

5. The skeleton protects soft body parts. _____

B. Complete the sentences. Use the words below.

bones	muscles	support
framework	protects	

1. The skeleton is like the _____ of a house.

2. The skeleton is made up of 206 _____.

3. Bones and _____ produce movement.

4. The skeleton _____ the soft parts of the body.

5. The body gets shape and _____ from the skeleton.

C. Use each word to write a sentence about the skeletal system.

1. skeleton _____

_____

2. bones _____

_____

D. Answer the questions.

1. What are two things your skeleton does for your body? _____

_____

_____

2. What parts of your body work together to help you move? _____

_____

3. What parts of your body are protected by the skeleton? _____

_____

The Parts of the Skeleton

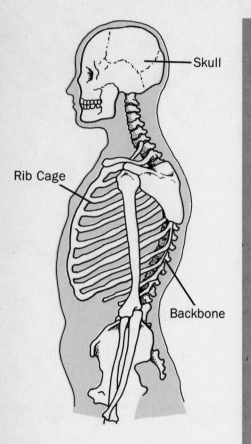

Skull

Rib Cage

Backbone

Bend forward and run your fingers down the middle of your back. Do you feel a line of bones? Each of the small bones you feel is called a **vertebra.** Many vertebrae are stacked on top of each other. This column of 26 vertebrae forms the **backbone.**

Each vertebra has a hole in the middle. The **spinal cord** goes through these holes. It is part of your nervous system. The spinal cord connects your brain with other parts of your body. An injury to the spinal cord could prevent parts of the body from moving. The important job of the backbone is to protect the spinal cord. (You will read more about the spinal cord and the nervous system later in this book.)

Attached to the backbone are 12 pairs of bones. These bones, or ribs, curve around the body. They form a kind of cage. The **rib cage** protects the heart and lungs. Ten of the bone pairs are attached to the breastbone at the front of the cage.

Another group of bones protects your eyes and brain. These bones form the **skull.** It may feel like one, large, round bone. But the skull is really made up of many bones. The bones of your face are also part of the skull.

A. Answer <u>True</u> or <u>False</u>.

1. The skull is shaped like a cage. _____

2. The backbone is made up of many vertebrae. _____

3. The brain is protected by the backbone. _____

4. The skull protects the brain. _____

5. The ribs protect the spinal cord. _____

6. The ribs are part of the skeletal system. _____

B. **Write the letter for the correct answer.**

1. A vertebra is part of the _____.
   (a) skull   (b) backbone   (c) rib cage

2. The ribs are attached to the _____.
   (a) skull   (b) brain   (c) backbone

3. A group of bones that protects the brain is the _____.
   (a) skull   (b) backbone   (c) rib cage

4. The backbone is made up of many _____.
   (a) cords   (b) ribs   (c) vertebrae

5. The part of the skeleton that protects the spinal cord is the _____.
   (a) rib cage   (b) skull   (c) backbone

6. The _____ is the part of the skeleton that protects the heart.
   (a) skull   (b) rib cage   (c) backbone

C. **Answer the questions.**

1. What is the important job of the rib cage? _____

   _____

2. What are the bones of the backbone called? _____

3. Name the important job of the skull. _____

   _____

4. What could happen if your spinal cord were injured? _____

   _____

5. What is the important job of the backbone? _____

   _____

Bones

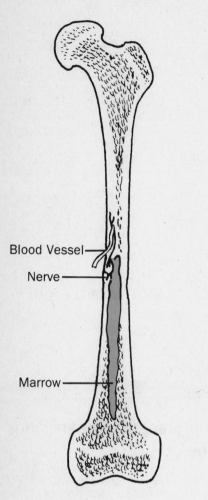

Blood Vessel

Nerve

Marrow

Inside a Bone

Bones are the hardest and the strongest parts of your body. You might think that bones don't grow or change. But like all the other parts of your body, bones are made of cells. When bone cells divide, bones grow longer. How can you tell that your bones have grown?

Bones can grow. They can also repair themselves. The outside of a bone is hard, but the inside is soft. Inside a bone are blood vessels and nerves. If a bone breaks, the bone repairs itself from the inside out. The blood vessels carry food into the bone. The food helps to build new bone.

Bone also contains a soft material called **marrow.** Red blood cells for the body are made in the marrow.

Not all parts of your body are shaped or supported by bone. Gently move the tip of your nose from side to side. Bend the tip of an ear forward. These parts of your body contain **cartilage.** Cartilage is part of your skeleton but it is softer than bone. It can bend without breaking. Cartilage supports your nose and ears. It is found between the vertebrae. The vertebrae are the bones of the backbone. Cartilage is also found where some bones come together. In all these places the cartilage acts as a cushion.

When you were born, almost all of your skeleton was made of soft, flexible cartilage. Within months, bones began to form from the cartilage. What parts of your skeleton never changed to bone?

A. Answer True or False.

1. Cartilage is harder than bone. _____

2. You have the same amount of cartilage in your body all your life. _____

3. Bones can repair themselves. _____

4. Red blood cells are made in marrow. _____

5. Bones always stay the same size. _____

6. Some cartilage changes to bone. _____

B. Complete the sentences. Use the words below.

blood vessels	cartilage	marrow
bones	cells	red blood cells

1. Bones can grow because they are made of _____.

2. The soft material inside a bone is _____.

3. When a bone breaks, _____ carry food into the bone.

4. Your nose and ears are supported by _____.

5. The bone marrow makes _____.

6. The hardest parts of your body are your _____.

C. Answer the questions.

1. What part of your skeleton can bend without breaking? _____

_____

2. What do blood vessels do in the bones? _____

_____

3. Where do new red blood cells come from? _____

4. What is a baby's skeleton made of? _____

5. What shapes and supports your arms and legs? _____

Joints

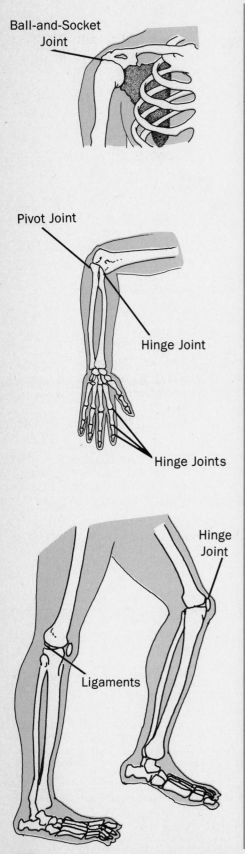

Ball-and-Socket Joint

Pivot Joint

Hinge Joint

Hinge Joints

Hinge Joint

Ligaments

You would not be able to move your body without **joints.** A joint is a place where two bones come together. At every joint, bones are held together by strong threadlike tissues called **ligaments.** Together, joints and ligaments let bones move.

There are three different kinds of moveable joints in the body. **Hinge joints** work like the hinge of a door. They can bend back and forth in only one direction. You have hinge joints in your elbows and knees. You also have hinge joints in your fingers and toes. These joints let you move all the many small bones in your hands and feet.

Your head is connected to your backbone by a **pivot joint.** A pivot joint can move around and back. This joint lets you twist your head around and look over your shoulder. You can also bend your head back or forward.

Remember that your elbow has a hinge joint. But it also has a pivot joint. This joint lets your arm twist so you can do things like turn a doorknob.

The joint that allows the most movement is a **ball-and-socket joint.** It can move in all directions. In a ball-and-socket joint, the end of one bone is shaped like a ball. It fits into a curved space at the end of the other bone. Your shoulders and hips have this kind of joint. A ball-and-socket joint can move in a complete circle. This lets you make the movements to throw a baseball or swim.

A. **Write the letter for the correct answer.**

1. Bones come together at _____ .
   (a) ligaments   (b) joints   (c) elbows

2. Hinge joints bend _____ .
   (a) in one direction   (b) in many directions   (c) all around

3. Your fingers have _____ .
   (a) hinge joints   (b) ball-and-socket joints   (c) no joints

4. Bones are held together by _____ .
   (a) blood vessels   (b) nerves   (c) ligaments

B. **Label the joints in the diagram.**

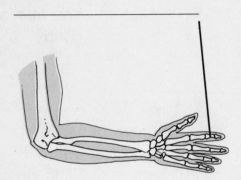
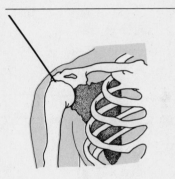

C. **Use each word to write a sentence about how your body moves.**

1. hinge joint _____

   _____

2. ball-and-socket joint _____

   _____

D. **Answer the questions.**

1. What tissues hold bones together? _____

2. How do hinge joints work? _____

   _____

3. What kind of joint can move in a complete circle? _____

   _____

Muscles That Move Bones

Shortened Muscle

Relaxed Muscle

Arm Bent

Relaxed Muscle

Shortened Muscle

Arm Straight

Your body has about 600 muscles. All these muscles working together form the **muscular system.** There are three kinds of muscle tissue in the system. One kind is **skeletal muscle.** Skeletal muscles move the bones of the skeleton. A second kind of muscle tissue is found in the heart. The third kind is found in the blood vessels and in organs like the stomach.

These three kinds of muscles are all made of cells. But they have three different jobs. Your skeletal muscles are under your control. You can control the muscles of your arm to lift your arm. But you cannot control the other kinds of muscle tissue in your body.

How do muscles move bones? A skeletal muscle gets shorter when it works. As it gets shorter, it pulls on the bone it is attached to. When a muscle stops working, it goes back to its regular size. By changing their length, muscles move the bones they are attached to.

Muscles are connected to bones by strong tissues called **tendons.** Tendons are like ligaments. But they do different jobs. Tendons connect muscles to bones. Ligaments connect bones to bones.

A. **Write the letter for the correct answer.**

1. The muscular system has _____ kinds of muscles.
   (a) two   (b) three   (c) ten

2. Muscles are made of _____ .
   (a) cells   (b) tendons   (c) ligaments.

3. When a muscle works, it gets _____.
   (a) softer   (b) longer   (c) shorter

4. Muscles are connected to bones by _____.
   (a) tendons   (b) ligaments   (c) organs

5. The bones of the skeleton are moved by _____.
   (a) heart muscles   (b) stomach muscles   (c) skeletal muscles

B. Answer True or False.

1. Muscles that move bones are the same as heart muscle. _____

2. Tendons connect muscles to bones. _____

3. Tendons and ligaments do the same job. _____

4. All muscles are made of cells. _____

C. Draw lines to complete the sentences.

1. Tendons   connect bones to bones.

2. Ligaments   three kinds of muscle.

3. Muscles   connect muscles to bones.

4. The muscular system has   move bones.

D. Answer the questions.

1. What are the three kinds of muscles? _____
   _____
   _____

2. What are muscles made of? _____

3. Which muscles can you control? _____

4. How are muscles connected to bones? _____
   _____

5. What happens to a muscle when it stops working? _____
   _____

Smooth Muscle and Heart Muscle

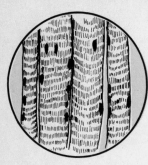
Skeletal Muscle

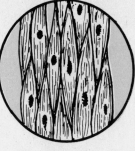
Smooth Muscle

Heart Muscle

How do you throw a ball or write your name? Your body uses more than 100 muscles to make these movements. But before you can move your arm you have to think about the motion. The skeletal muscles move because your brain tells them to move. That is why the skeletal muscles that move the bones of your body are called **voluntary muscles.**

You have two other kinds of muscles in your body. They are **smooth muscle** and **heart muscle.** The three kinds of muscle look different from each other. They also have different jobs to do.

Smooth muscles are found in large blood vessels. They help control the flow of blood through the vessels. Smooth muscles are also important in digesting food. They move the walls of the stomach so that food is mixed with stomach juices. Smooth muscles also help move wastes through the large intestine.

Heart muscles have a very special job to do. They make your heart beat and pump blood to other parts of the body. Heart muscles work all the time, even when you are sleeping.

Smooth muscles and heart muscles are different from skeletal muscles in another important way. They are **involuntary muscles.** You do not control them. You do not have to think about digesting your food. Your stomach muscles do their job. You do not have to think about your heart to keep it pumping.

A. Answer <u>True</u> or <u>False</u>.

1. Skeletal muscles are involuntary. _____

2. Digesting food is involuntary. _____

3. The brain tells voluntary muscles what to do. _____

4. Smooth muscles move bones. _____

5. Thinking can control the heart muscles. _____

B. Label the diagrams.

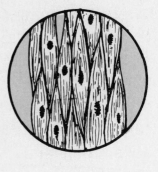  

_____   _____   _____

C. Write two ways that smooth muscles and heart muscles are different from skeletal muscles.

_____

_____

_____

D. Answer the questions.

1. What are two jobs that smooth muscles do? _____

_____

2. Which muscles are called voluntary muscles? _____

_____

3. What do heart muscles do? _____

_____

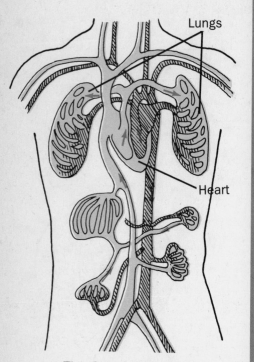

Lungs

Heart

The Circulatory System

Blood travels through the body. It carries important materials that all of the body cells need. How do you think blood gets from one part of the body to another?

Blood is one part of the **circulatory system.** The other two parts of the system are the heart and the blood vessels. All the parts of the circulatory system have important jobs. The heart is the pump that keeps blood moving. The blood vessels are the paths the blood takes. The vessels can be large or small.

Blood moves through the circulatory system. It carries food and oxygen to the body cells. Inside the cells, food and oxygen mix to release the energy needed for life.

As they make energy, cells also make wastes. One of these wastes is a gas called carbon dioxide. The blood carries carbon dioxide away from the cells. If wastes were not removed, the body would be poisoned.

The circulatory system helps protect the body from disease. Certain cells and chemicals can fight the germs that cause disease. The blood carries these germ fighters to the part of the body where they are needed.

When you exercise, you may begin to feel warm. Your circulatory system helps to keep you cool. Blood takes heat away from your organs. It carries the heat to your skin. The heat can then leave your body through your skin.

A. Answer True or False.

1. The circulatory system has three parts. _____

2. The circulatory system helps protect the body from disease.

_____

3. Oxygen is a waste made by cells. _____

4. Blood moves through blood vessels. _____

B. Complete the sentences. Use the words below.

blood	cell	oxygen
carbon dioxide	heart	

1. The _____ is the pump that keeps blood moving.

2. The circulatory system delivers food and _____ to the cells.

3. The blood takes the gas _____ away from the cells.

4. Germ fighters are carried by the _____ .

5. Blood must reach each _____ in every part of the body.

C. Use each word to write a sentence about the circulatory system.

1. oxygen _____

_____

2. germ fighters _____

_____

D. Answer the questions.

1. How do body cells get food and oxygen? _____

_____

2. Why is it important for wastes to be carried away from cells? ____

_____

Blood Vessels

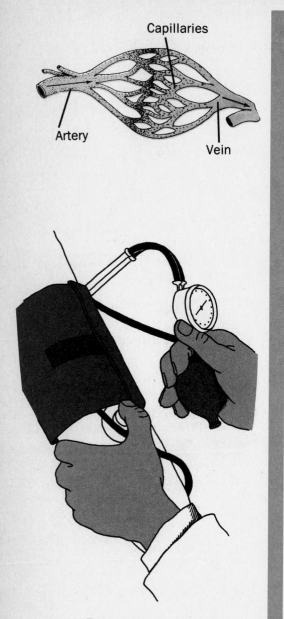

Capillaries

Artery

Vein

Taking Blood Pressure

Think of the circulatory system as a delivery service. Then you can think of the **blood vessels** as roads. Blood vessels come in different sizes. Some are large. They are like highways. Others are smaller. They are like wide and narrow streets.

The largest blood vessels are called **arteries.** Arteries carry blood away from the heart. The blood they carry is rich in oxygen.

Arteries divide into smaller and smaller blood vessels. The smallest blood vessels are called **capillaries.** The blood in the capillaries is carrying food and oxygen. These materials pass through the thin walls of the capillaries. They move into the body cells. The body cells take the food and oxygen they need. Then the blood moves back into the capillaries.

From the capillaries, the blood moves into **veins.** Veins are larger than capillaries but smaller than arteries. They bring blood back to the heart. The blood they carry has lost its food and oxygen. In the heart and lungs the blood gets a new supply of food and oxygen. It also loses the wastes it is carrying.

The pumping of blood pushes the blood against the walls of the blood vessels. This push is called **blood pressure.** If arteries are blocked with fat, the heart has to pump harder to push the blood through. This is called high blood pressure. It can be dangerous to your health.

A. Answer True or False.

1. Blood in the arteries is rich in oxygen. _____

2. Capillaries are the largest vessels. _____

3. Veins are smaller than arteries. _____

4. The push of blood is called blood pressure. _____

5. High blood pressure can be dangerous to your health. _____

B. Complete the sentences. Use the words below.

arteries	blood pressure	capillaries	veins

1. The smallest blood vessels are the _____.

2. The largest blood vessels are the _____.

3. Blood vessels that bring blood back to the heart are _____.

4. The push of blood against the walls of blood vessels is

   _____.

C. Answer the questions.

1. Are all blood vessels the same size? _____

   _____

2. Which type of blood vessel carries blood away from the heart? ____

   _____

3. Which blood vessels do body cells get food and oxygen from? ____

   _____

4. What happens to blood pressure when arteries are blocked with fat?

   _____

5. Where does blood get a new supply of food and oxygen? ____

   _____

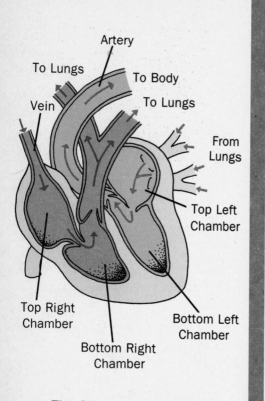

Artery
To Lungs
To Body
To Lungs
Vein
From Lungs
Top Left Chamber
Top Right Chamber
Bottom Left Chamber
Bottom Right Chamber

The Circulation of Blood Through the Heart

The **heart** is the most important organ in your body. It is not much larger than a fist. Your heart is really a double pump. The two pumps are separated by a wall of tissue that runs down the middle of the heart. Each side of the heart is divided into two **chambers.** Blood moves through the four chambers of the heart.

After it has traveled through the body, blood enters the top right chamber. This blood is carrying wastes from the cells. From the top right chamber the blood goes through a **valve** to the bottom right chamber. A valve is a flap of tissue that opens and closes. But it only lets blood flow in one direction.

The bottom right chamber pumps blood to the lungs. In the lungs, the blood drops off carbon dioxide. It picks up oxygen.

From the lungs, the blood carrying the oxygen goes back to the heart. It enters the top left chamber. Then it passes through a valve into the bottom left chamber. This chamber pumps blood to the rest of the body.

The left side of the heart works harder than the right side. It has to pump blood to all parts of the body, except the lungs. The right side of the heart pumps blood only to the lungs.

When you are exercising, your body needs more food and oxygen than normal. So your heart beats faster. When you are sleeping, your heart beats more slowly. But your heart never stops. It began to beat before you were born and it keeps on beating your whole life.

A. Answer True or False.

1. There are four chambers in the heart. _____

2. Valves in the heart let blood travel in all directions. _____

3. The right side of the heart sends blood to the lungs. _____

4. The blood that enters the top right chamber contains wastes from the cells. _____

B. Draw lines to complete the sentences.

1. The heart   more slowly during sleep.

2. The heart beats   works all the time.

3. Valves   four chambers.

4. The heart has   let blood pass from one chamber to another.

C. Number the sentences to show how blood flows through the heart.

_____ Blood goes through a valve to the bottom right chamber.

_____ Blood enters the top left chamber.

_____ The bottom right chamber pumps blood to the lungs.

___1___ After traveling through the body, blood enters the top right chamber.

_____ The bottom left chamber pumps blood to the rest of the body.

D. Answer the questions.

1. How big is your heart? _____

2. Why does the left side of the heart work harder than the right side?

_____

_____

3. Why does the heart beat faster when you are exercising? _____

_____

The Blood

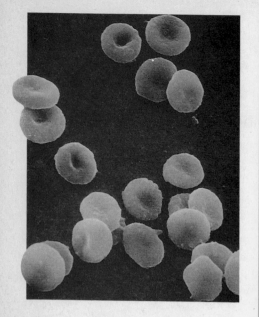

Red Blood Cells

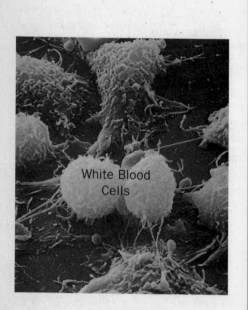

White Blood
Cells

White Blood Cells

When you cut yourself you see the bright red liquid called **blood.** Blood is made of both liquids and solids. About half of blood is liquid.

The liquid part of blood is called **plasma.** Ninety percent of plasma is water. Plasma holds the food that the blood delivers to cells. It also carries the wastes made by the cells. Plasma is also the part of the blood that brings germ fighters to the places in the body where they are needed.

Remember that **red blood cells** are made in bone marrow. These cells float in the plasma. They are shaped like circles with a dent in the middle. They are so small that they can fit through a tiny capillary.

The red blood cells are the part of the blood that carries oxygen to body cells. To do their job, red blood cells need **iron.** Iron is a mineral. It is found in dark green vegetables, grains, and liver. Why is it a good idea to eat these foods?

Another type of cell is found in the plasma. These are **white blood cells.** White blood cells are much larger than red blood cells. But there are not as many of these cells. In fact, for every white blood cell in the body, there are 700 red blood cells.

White blood cells help the body fight germs that can cause disease. Have you ever seen pus in a cut or a wound? Pus is made of dead germs and white blood cells. The pus shows that the white blood cells are doing their job.

A. Answer True or False.

1. Plasma is ninety percent water. _____

2. There are very few red blood cells in the body. _____

3. White blood cells are germ fighters. _____

4. Red blood cells are made in the plasma. _____

B. Write the letter for the correct answer.

1. The liquid part of blood is _____.
   (a) cells   (b) pus   (c) plasma

2. Food for the cells is carried by _____.
   (a) marrow   (b) plasma   (c) vessels

3. _____ bring oxygen to body cells.
   (a) Red blood cells   (b) White blood cells   (c) Minerals

4. _____ are germ fighters.
   (a) Red blood cells   (b) White blood cells   (c) Food particles

5. _____ helps red blood cells do their job.
   (a) Pus   (b) Plasma   (c) Iron

6. Most of the plasma is _____.
   (a) water   (b) iron   (c) minerals

C. Answer the questions.

1. What does plasma do? Name three things. _____

   _____

   _____

   _____

2. What part of the blood carries oxygen to the body cells? _____

   _____

3. What part of the blood fights germs? _____

   _____

Keeping Systems Healthy

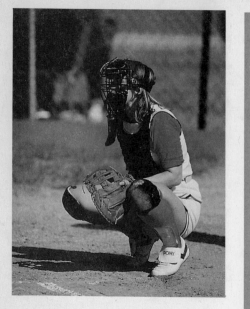

Wear the right protective gear for any game you play.

Your body systems work best when they are healthy. How can you take care of them?

If you play sports, protect your bones and ligaments. Wear a helmet to protect your skull if you play football. Also wear any other protective gear suggested for the sports you play.

Keep your bones strong by eating foods that contain calcium. These foods include milk products. Protein foods are important, too. Proteins are found in eggs, meat, beans, and milk products.

A good diet will also help keep your muscular system healthy. So will the proper amount of rest and exercise. Walking is one form of good exercise.

Rest, exercise, and a good diet are also important for your circulatory system. Eating foods high in salt or fats can cause high blood pressure. High blood pressure can lead to a heart attack.

A. Answer <u>True</u> or <u>False</u>.

1. Wearing protective gear for sports can prevent injury. _____

2. Foods high in fat protect the circulatory system. _____

B. Answer the questions.

1. Why is it important to eat foods that contain calcium and protein?

   _____

2. How can you care for your muscular system? _____

   _____

36

Review

Part A

Read each sentence. Write <u>True</u> if the sentence is true and <u>False</u> if the sentence is false.

1. Bones in the skeleton protect the soft parts of the body. _____

2. Bones do not grow or change. _____

3. All joints move in the same way. _____

4. Heart muscles are under your control. _____

5. Carbon dioxide is a waste made by cells. _____

6. Arteries carry blood rich in food and oxygen. _____

7. The heart has four chambers. _____

8. White blood cells help fight germs. _____

Part B

Complete the sentences. Use the words below.

backbone	joints	plasma
cartilage	ligaments	red blood cells
exercise	oxygen	skeleton

1. The human body is supported by a _____.

2. The part of the skeleton that protects the spinal cord is the

   _____.

3. The soft parts of the skeleton are made of _____.

4. Bones are held together by _____.

5. Your bones meet at places called _____.

6. The liquid part of blood is called _____.

7. The parts of the blood that carry oxygen are _____.

8. To stay healthy, body systems need good food, rest, and _____.

Fill in the circle in front of the word or phrase that best completes the sentence. The first one is done for you.

1. The bones of the skeleton
   ● store minerals.
   ⓑ pump blood.
   ⓒ move by themselves.

2. The vertebrae in the backbone
   ⓐ are muscles.
   ⓑ protect the spinal cord.
   ⓒ are part of the circulatory system.

3. Cartilage is
   ⓐ harder than bone.
   ⓑ softer than bone.
   ⓒ made by marrow.

4. Joints and ligaments
   ⓐ are found in the brain.
   ⓑ make red blood cells.
   ⓒ let bones move.

5. Tendons connect muscles to
   ⓐ ligaments.
   ⓑ bones.
   ⓒ tissues.

6. Breathing is
   ⓐ involuntary.
   ⓑ voluntary.
   ⓒ controlled by the heart.

7. Cells produce energy from
   ⓐ muscles.
   ⓑ oxygen and food.
   ⓒ carbon dioxide.

8. Blood moves through the body in
   ⓐ bones.
   ⓑ blood vessels.
   ⓒ muscles.

9. The heart has four
   ⓐ pumps.
   ⓑ chambers.
   ⓒ valves.

10. Red blood cells
    ⓐ fight germs.
    ⓑ carry waste.
    ⓒ carry oxygen.

Fill in the missing word in each sentence. Use the words below.

---

blood	joints	smooth
bones	ligaments	system
diet	plasma	veins
involuntary	skeletal	

Red ◯ _ _ _ _ cells are made in bone marrow.

_ _ ◯ _ _ _ muscles are found in large blood vessels.

A good ◯ _ _ _ is important for healthy body systems.

_ _ _ _ _ _ _ _ _ _ _ ◯ muscles are always at work in the heart.

The ◯ _ _ _ _ _ _ _ muscles move bones.

The circulatory _ ◯ _ _ _ _ carries food and oxygen to all body cells.

_ _ _ ◯ _ _ is mostly water.

_ _ _ _ ◯ _ are where bones come together.

_ ◯ _ _ _ carry blood without food or oxygen.

_ _ _ _ ◯ _ _ _ connect bones to bones.

_ _ _ _ _ ◯ shape and support your body.

Write each circled letter on a space below. What do the letters spell?

_ _ _ _ _   _ _ _ _ _ _ _

The Digestive System

Nutrients

Food. It can be crunchy or soft. It can be sweet or sour. You can pick it off a tree or buy it in a store. It may be fresh, frozen, or come in cans and boxes. There is a lot of food to choose from. But what kind of food is good for you?

Your body needs certain raw materials to move, grow, and repair itself. These raw materials are called **nutrients.** Nutrients are the parts of food your body can use.

Two different foods can contain the same nutrient. For example, both cheeses and meats contain **proteins.** Your body needs proteins to grow. It uses proteins to repair body tissue. Proteins are found in fish and milk. Eggs, peas, and some kinds of beans are good sources of protein, too.

Another nutrient needed by your body is **carbohydrates.** Carbohydrates are either starches or sugars. Your body uses carbohydrates to produce energy. Fruits, breads, cereals, pasta, and most vegetables contain carbohydrates. If you eat more carbohydrates than you need, your body stores them as fat.

Like carbohydrates, **fats** give your body energy. Fats are important nutrients. But you should not eat more fats than you need. Meats, cheeses, and butter have fat. But it is healthier to get fats from vegetable sources. These include nuts, corn oil, and soybean oil.

To stay healthy, find out which nutrients your food contains.

A. Fill in the missing word.

1. The raw materials your body needs are called _____.
   (cells, nutrients)

2. Both cheeses and meats contain _____. (milk, proteins)

3. Sugar is a kind of _____. (carbohydrate, protein)

4. For energy, your body uses _____.
   (bones, carbohydrates)

5. Proteins are found in milk and _____. (water, fish)

B. Answer True or False.

1. Two different foods can contain the same nutrient. _____

2. Nutrients are the part of food your body has to get rid of. _____

3. Your body needs proteins to grow and repair body tissue. _____

4. Fats do not supply energy to your body. _____

5. Nuts and oils have fats. _____

C. Write the letter for the correct answer.

1. Your body uses the _____ from food.
   (a) fruits   (b) nutrients   (c) waste

2. It is healthier to get most of your fats from _____.
   (a) sugars   (b) vegetable sources   (c) meat

3. If you eat too many carbohydrates, your body will store them

   as _____.
   (a) blood   (b) fat   (c) sugar

4. A food that contains proteins is _____.
   (a) fruit   (b) water   (c) milk

5. Breads and pasta are sources of _____.
   (a) carbohydrates   (b) fats   (c) proteins

6. Carbohydrates are either starches or _____.
   (a) salts   (b) sugars   (c) fats

Vitamins and Minerals

Getting the right amounts of carbohydrates, fats, and proteins can keep you healthy. But these three nutrients need help to do their jobs correctly. They get the help they need from two other nutrients, **vitamins** and **minerals.**

Vitamins and minerals help other nutrients do their jobs in three important ways. First, they control the way your body uses carbohydrates for energy. They also control how fast cells grow. Vitamins and minerals keep all body systems working smoothly.

The table below shows some important vitamins and minerals. It tells which foods contain these vitamins. It also explains what the vitamins and minerals can do.

VITAMINS	Needed for	Sources
A	Healthy skin, eyes, and teeth	Vegetables, eggs, liver
B	Making red blood cells, using food for energy	Vegetables, nuts, grains, meats
C	Healthy teeth, gums, and blood vessels	Citrus fruits, tomatoes
D	Healthy bones and teeth	Milk, fish, liver

MINERALS	Needed for	Sources
Iron	Healthy red blood cells	Green vegetables, meat, raisins
Calcium	Strong bones	Green vegetables, milk, fish
Sodium	Correct amount of water in the body	Meat, cheese, salt
Zinc	Repairing tissue	Fish, meat, grains, beans

A. Use the table of vitamins and minerals to answer the questions.

1. Vitamins and _____ help other nutrients do their jobs. (minerals, fats)

2. Vitamin C can be found in _____. (nuts, citrus fruits)

3. If you want healthy red blood cells, eat foods rich in the mineral _____. (liver, iron)

4. For healthy skin, eyes, and teeth, eat foods rich in _____. (vitamin A, sodium)

5. Calcium is found in _____. (raisins, milk)

B. Answer the questions.

1. Name three things that vitamins and minerals can do.

   _____

   _____

   _____

2. List two foods that contain vitamin A.

   _____

   _____

3. Name three body parts that need vitamin C to stay healthy.

   _____

   _____

   _____

C. Underline the answer to each question.

1. Which two nutrients help other nutrients?
   (vitamins and minerals, fats and sugars)

2. Which vitamin keeps your gums healthy? (sodium, vitamin C)

3. Which food contains vitamin B? (raisins, grains)

4. Which mineral grows strong bones? (vitamin A, calcium)

Food Groups and a Balanced Diet

Meat Group

Dairy Group

Vegetable and Fruit Group

Cereal and Bread Group

How do you get the nutrients you need from food? The best way is to divide food into **four basic food groups.** Eat foods from the four groups every day. The four basic food groups are: **meat; dairy; vegetables and fruit;** and **cereals and breads.**

Eating meat and other foods from the meat group, such as fish, nuts, and beans, will give you proteins, vitamins, and minerals. Try to have at least 2 servings from the meat group each day.

Dairy foods include milk and milk products, such as yogurt and cheese. These foods supply proteins, vitamins A, B, and D, calcium, and fats. Try to eat dairy foods 2 to 4 times each day.

Vegetables and fruits are rich in many nutrients. Fresh vegetables and fruits have more nutrients than those that are frozen or in cans. Eat 4 or more servings of fruits and vegetables every day.

Cereals and breads have B vitamins, iron, carbohydrates, and some proteins. Try to eat these foods 4 times a day.

Eating daily from all four food groups will give you a **balanced diet.** Suppose a person doesn't have a balanced diet. Without enough carbohydrates a person might lose weight and feel tired. A lack of protein slows down growth and makes muscles weaker. A person may not have much energy. Without enough vitamins or minerals, teeth and bones can lose their strength. Also, a person may not be able to fight off certain diseases.

A. **Answer True or False.**

1. There are nine basic food groups. _____

2. Eating meat once a week is enough for a balanced diet. _____

3. Eating foods from one food group will keep you healthy. _____

4. Fats are one of the food groups. _____

B. **Draw lines between the food and the group it belongs to.**

1. fish   dairy

2. cheese   vegetables and fruits

3. carrots   cereals and breads

4. oatmeal   meat

C. **Fill in the missing word.**

1. Dairy foods supply _____. (proteins, cereals)

2. Vegetables and fruits contain many different kinds of _____. (calcium, vitamins)

3. Eat cereals and breads at least _____ times a day. (4, 8)

4. Meat is a good source of _____. (sugar, protein)

D. **Answer the questions.**

1. List the basic food groups.

   _____   _____

   _____   _____

2. How can a lack of protein affect a person? _____

   _____

   _____

3. How can a lack of vitamins or minerals affect a person? _____

   _____

   _____

Calories

FOOD CALORIES	
apple	80
baked potato	145
banana	100
bread (1 slice)	80
butter (1 Tbsp.)	100
cheddar cheese (1 oz.)	115
chicken (3 oz.)	115
cola (12 oz.)	145
egg (hard boiled)	80
green beans (1 cup)	30
ground beef (3 oz.)	220
ice cream (1 cup)	275
lowfat milk (1 cup)	120
mayonnaise (1 Tbsp.)	100
oatmeal (1 cup)	130
orange	65
peanuts (½ cup)	420
potato chips (10)	115
tomato	25
tuna (3 oz.)	170
yogurt (8 oz.)	145

You get energy from the food you eat. The energy in food is measured in **calories.** Some foods have more calories than others. A tomato has about 25 calories. A cup of ice cream has about 275 calories. You could eat 11 tomatoes to equal the number of calories in a cup of ice cream!

Your body uses calories for all its activities. Every time your hand moves or your heart beats, some calories are used. What happens if your body does not use all the calories in the food you eat? Then the unused calories are stored as fat.

How many calories you need depends upon the amount of energy your body needs. If you are active, then your body needs lots of energy. The calories you take in will be used up. You can eat a lot without getting fat.

If you are not very active, your body needs less energy. If you eat a lot, all the calories in your food may not get used up. Your body will store the calories as fat.

There are two things you can do to lose extra fat. You can exercise to use more calories. Or you can cut down on high-calorie foods. That way your body will have fewer calories to use. But using both methods is the best way to lose weight.

Whether you need to lose weight or not, stay away from empty calories. Empty calories are found in foods that are high in calories but low in vitamins and minerals. Candy, soft drinks, and other "junk" foods are empty-calorie foods.

A. Write the letter for the correct answer.

1. The number of calories you need depends upon _____ .
   (a) the energy you need   (b) your bones   (c) your heart

2. Candy and soft drinks contain _____ .
   (a) many nutrients   (b) empty calories   (c) all you need

3. Unused calories are stored as _____ .
   (a) sugar   (b) bone   (c) fat

4. A person can lose weight by _____ .
   (a) eating "junk" food   (b) exercising   (c) being less active

B. Answer True or False.

1. The energy you get from food is measured in calories. _____

2. All foods have the same number of calories. _____

3. Every activity you do uses up calories. _____

4. Empty-calorie foods are high in vitamins. _____

C. Choose the correct answer.

1. "Junk" food is food with _____ .
   (empty calories, nutrients)

2. You can lose weight by cutting down on _____ .
   (protein, high-calorie foods)

3. Active bodies need a lot of _____ . (energy, candy)

4. Exercising more makes your body use more _____ .
   (vitamins, calories)

D. Answer the questions.

1. What do calories measure? _____

   _____

2. What happens if your body does not use all the calories you take in?

   _____

How Digestion Begins

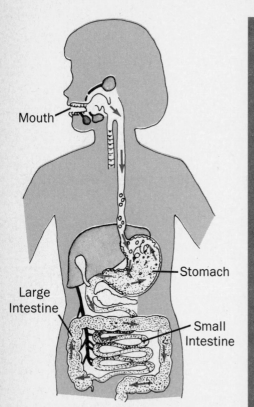

Mouth

Stomach

Large Intestine

Small Intestine

The Digestive System

How does the body take what it needs from food? The body gets its raw materials from food by the process of **digestion.** Digestion is the breaking down of food into nutrients.

The nutrients from food go into the blood. The blood carries the nutrients to all the body cells. Body cells use the nutrients to produce energy. The part of the food that the body cannot use is removed from the body. How does food travel through your body?

Your **digestive system** is like a long tube. As food moves through the tube, it is changed by different organs. First, some organs grind up the food. Then others change it by mixing it with chemicals. Next, other organs move the nutrients from the food into the blood. Finally, the unused part of the food is sent out of the body. The main organs of the digestive system are the **mouth,** the **stomach,** the **small intestine,** and the **large intestine.**

Food enters your body through your mouth. As your teeth grind up the food, it mixes with a liquid called **saliva.**

Saliva contains a chemical that can change starch into sugar. Once the starch in your food has become sugar, it can pass into the blood. Then the body can use the sugar to make energy.

When food leaves your mouth, it is still not completely digested. More starch needs to be changed into sugar. Proteins and fats have to be broken down. Digestion continues in the stomach.

A. Complete each sentence. Use the words below.

digestion	nutrients	saliva
mouth	organ	sugar

1. The body gets its raw materials from food by the process of

   _____ .

2. Food enters your body through your _____ .

3. The liquid in your mouth is called _____ .

4. Saliva contains a chemical that changes starch into _____ .

5. Digestion is the breaking down of food into _____ .

B. Answer True or False.

1. Digestion helps grind food into smaller pieces. _____

2. The small intestine is an organ of the digestive system. _____

3. In the digestive system, food is mixed with chemicals. _____

4. Every part of food is used by the body. _____

5. When food leaves the mouth, it is completely digested. _____

C. Number the sentences to show what happens to food during digestion. The first one is done for you.

_____ Nutrients from the food go into the blood.

___1___ Food is ground up.

_____ Food is mixed with chemicals.

_____ The unused part of food is sent out of the body.

D. List the four main organs of the digestive system.

_____   _____

_____   _____

49

Digestion Continues

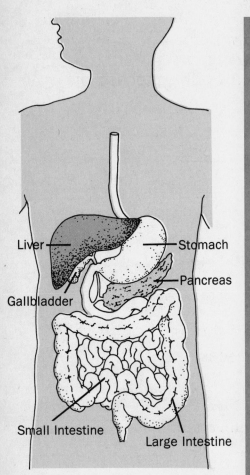

The Digestive System

Liver

Stomach

Pancreas

Gallbladder

Small Intestine

Large Intestine

In the stomach, more chemicals are mixed with food. Stomach juices begin to break down proteins. Stomach muscles act like a blender to mix the food. By the time the food leaves the stomach, it has become a liquid.

Now is the time for the most important step of digestion. The partly digested food moves from the stomach into the small intestine. The small intestine is like a hose. If it were stretched out straight, it would be about 20 feet long.

As food moves slowly along this "hose," its nutrients pass through the walls of the small intestine. These walls are lined with tiny blood vessels. Like water soaking into a sponge, the nutrients pass into the tiny blood vessels. Then the blood carries the nutrients to every cell in the body.

The process of digestion is helped by other organs. The **liver** and the **gallbladder** pump chemicals into the small intestine. These chemicals help break down fats. The **pancreas** pumps in other chemicals. These chemicals break down fats as well as proteins and starches.

When too much sugar is produced during digestion, the body has to store it. This is another job of the liver. It stores sugar that the body does not need.

Eventually, the food that is left passes out of the small intestine. It moves into the large intestine. From here it will be carried out of the body.

A. Write the letter for the correct answer.

1. By the time food has left the stomach, it is already _____.
   (a) completely digested   (b) a liquid   (c) energy

2. The organ that helps store extra sugar is the _____.
   (a) liver   (b) stomach   (c) mouth

3. Juices in the stomach help break down _____.
   (a) proteins   (b) fruit   (c) water

4. In the small intestine, nutrients pass into _____.
   (a) the stomach   (b) blood vessels   (c) the food

B. Answer True or False.

1. Stomach muscles act like a blender to mix food. _____

2. Food passes from the stomach into the large intestine. _____

3. Blood carries digested food to all parts of the body. _____

C. Put the main organs of the digestive system in the correct order.

stomach   _____

mouth   _____

large intestine   _____

small intestine   _____

D. Answer the questions.

1. What happens to nutrients in the small intestine? _____

_____

_____

2. What happens to food that is not digested in the small intestine?

_____

_____

3. Name two jobs of the liver. _____

_____

Solid Waste

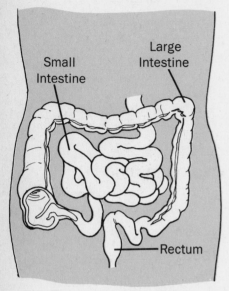

The excretory system removes solid waste.

Once food leaves the small intestine, most of its usable parts have been removed. Only waste products and extra water are left. The job of the **excretory system** is to remove waste from the body.

The undigested food moves from the small intestine into the large intestine. Some water is removed for use by the body. The solid waste is pushed through the large intestine by muscles.

In the large intestine, tiny organisms called **bacteria** begin to feed on the waste. Bacteria break down the waste.

Finally, the waste reaches the end of the large intestine. It passes through the last part of the digestive system. This is known as the **rectum.** Muscles in the rectum push waste out of the body.

A. Choose the correct answer.

1. After food leaves the small intestine, only _____ and water are left. (nutrients, waste)

2. The _____ is the last part of the digestive system. (rectum, small intestine)

3. In the large intestine, organisms called _____ feed on waste. (bacteria, nutrients)

B. Answer <u>True</u> or <u>False</u>.

1. Muscles in the rectum push waste out of the body. _____

2. In the large intestine, some of the water is removed from food for use by the body. _____

52

The Excretory System

Liquid Waste

Remember that your body needs to get rid of undigested food. The excretory system removes this solid waste from the body. But the body also needs a way to get rid of harmful chemicals. And it has to remove extra water. This liquid waste is also removed by the excretory system.

The main organs of the excretory system are the **kidneys.** The kidneys are two bean-shaped organs about the size of your fist. The kidneys act as filters. As blood passes through them, the kidneys filter out water, salts, and harmful chemicals. The liquid that is produced is called **urine.**

Urine moves from the kidneys to the **bladder.** When your bladder is full, you feel the need to empty it. Then urine passes from your bladder out of the body.

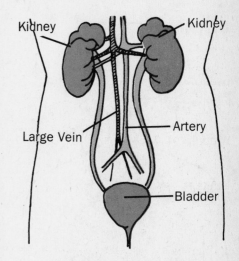

Kidney | Kidney
Large Vein | Artery
Bladder

The excretory system removes liquid waste.

A. Answer True or False.

1. Your body saves every part of the food you eat. _____

2. Liquid waste is filtered through the kidneys. _____

B. Choose the correct answer.

1. The main organs of the excretory system are the _____.
    (kidneys, bladder)

2. The liquid waste of the body is _____. (water, urine)

3. Liquid waste moves from the kidneys to the _____.
    (bladder, intestine)

4. Along with water, urine also contains _____. (food, salts)

Taking in Air

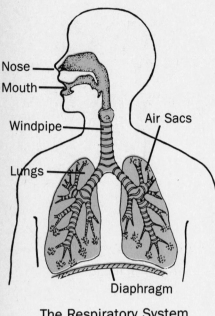

Nose
Mouth
Windpipe
Air Sacs
Lungs
Diaphragm

The Respiratory System

All your body cells need oxygen. Without oxygen, your body cells cannot produce energy. The organs of your **respiratory system** bring oxygen into your body for your cells. They also get rid of the wastes given off by the cells. The main organs of the respiratory system are the **lungs.** How does the respiratory system work?

To breathe you need the help of your muscular system. A large muscle called the **diaphragm** controls your lungs. When the diaphragm moves down, air is pulled into the lungs. When the diaphragm moves up, air is forced out of the lungs.

Air usually enters the body through the nose. Inside the nose, tiny hairs clean the air by catching dirt and other particles. The air is also warmed as it travels through the nose.

The clean warm air moves into a tube in your throat called the **windpipe.** The air is warmed still more in this tube. The windpipe divides into two smaller tubes. Each tube goes into one of the lungs.

The tubes continue to divide in the lungs. They get smaller and smaller and end in tiny **air sacs.** The lungs are made up of about 300 million of these air sacs.

A. Choose the correct answer.

1. Breathing brings _____ into the body. (oxygen, nutrients)

2. The lungs are controlled by a muscle known as the _____. (diaphragm, windpipe)

3. Air is _____ in the windpipe. (cooled, warmed)

4. Air moves from the nose to the _____. (lungs, windpipe)

B. Answer True or False.

1. The cells in your body need oxygen to produce energy. _____

2. When the diaphragm moves down, air is forced into the lungs.

   _____

3. Air enters the body through the lungs. _____

C. Write the letter for the correct answer.

1. The body needs oxygen to make _____.
   (a) blood   (b) bones   (c) energy

2. The main organs of the respiratory system are the _____.
   (a) lungs   (b) muscles   (c) diaphragm

3. After the nose, the air enters the _____.
   (a) windpipe   (b) diaphragm   (c) blood

4. The lungs are controlled by _____.
   (a) the diaphragm   (b) air   (c) the nose

5. The lungs are made up of many _____.
   (a) bones   (b) air sacs   (c) hairs

D. Answer the questions.

1. What is the job of the respiratory system? _____

   _____

   _____

2. What two things happen to air inside the nose? _____

   _____

3. What are the lungs made of? _____

   _____

Exchanging Gases

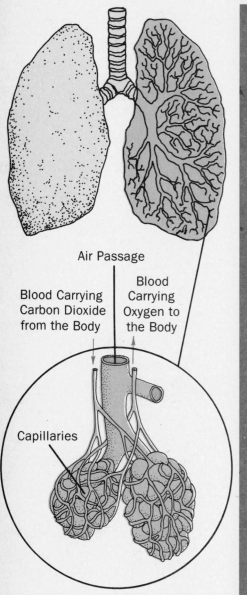

Air Passage

Blood Carrying Carbon Dioxide from the Body

Blood Carrying Oxygen to the Body

Capillaries

Oxygen and carbon dioxide are exchanged in the air sacs of the lungs.

The tiniest tubes of the lungs end in millions of tiny air sacs. Air sacs are like little balloons. Each sac is surrounded by many capillaries.

When you breathe in, oxygen enters the air sacs. The oxygen passes through the thin walls of the air sacs and enters the capillaries. Then the oxygen is picked up by red blood cells. The blood cells carry oxygen to every cell in the body.

At the same time, another process is taking place. Carbon dioxide from the blood moves out of the capillaries. It moves into the air sacs. Then the carbon dioxide leaves your body as you breathe out. Remember that carbon dioxide is a waste produced by all body cells. It is produced when body cells break down food and give off energy.

In the lungs, carbon dioxide and oxygen are exchanged all the time. Your body depends on this process to stay alive. If your body did not get enough oxygen, its cells would soon die. The cells would also die if they could not get rid of carbon dioxide. The carbon dioxide would build up in the blood and become poisonous.

A. **Answer True or False.**

1. There are only a few air sacs in each lung. _____

2. Air sacs are surrounded by capillaries. _____

3. In the lungs, oxygen is picked up by carbon dioxide. _____

4. Carbon dioxide is a waste product. _____

5. When you breathe out, carbon dioxide leaves your body. _____

6. Not getting enough oxygen could kill your body cells. _____

7. Carbon dioxide building up in your blood is not harmful. _____

8. In your lungs, oxygen and carbon dioxide are exchanged. _____

B. Write the letter for the correct answer.

1. The smallest tubes in the lungs end in _____.
   (a) windpipes   (b) air sacs   (c) vessels

2. Oxygen reaching the air sacs is picked up by _____.
   (a) red blood cells   (b) carbon dioxide   (c) water

3. All body cells produce a waste product called _____.
   (a) oxygen   (b) carbon dioxide   (c) blood

4. Without enough oxygen, your cells would _____.
   (a) divide   (b) get smaller   (c) die

5. Carbon dioxide moves out of capillaries and into the _____.
   (a) body cells   (b) air sacs   (c) red blood cells

C. Answer the questions.

1. Describe the air sacs of the lungs. _____

   _____

2. How does oxygen get to every cell in the body? _____

   _____

   _____

3. How does carbon dioxide leave the blood? _____

   _____

   _____

4. What would happen if your body cells could not get rid of carbon

   dioxide? _____

   _____

57

Eating vegetables helps the body get rid of solid waste.

Keep your digestive system in working order by drinking lots of liquids. Take care of your teeth, too. You need strong teeth to chew food.

Your body loses a lot of water through sweat and urine. So taking in liquids is also important for your excretory system. Eating fruits, vegetables, and grains helps the body get rid of solid wastes.

Your respiratory system needs strong muscles and healthy lungs to bring lots of oxygen into the body. Exercising helps to strengthen the muscles you use to breathe. It also makes your lungs work harder.

Last of all, don't smoke. Smoking harms the tissues of the lungs. Damaged lungs cannot bring your cells all the oxygen they need.

A. **Answer True or False.**

1. Drinking a lot of liquids is good for your digestion. _____

2. Smoking damages the lungs. _____

3. Exercising is bad for your lungs. _____

B. **Name the body systems helped by each of the following.**

1. Not smoking _____

2. Caring for teeth _____

3. Drinking liquids _____

Review

Part A

Read the descriptions below. Then choose the word that best matches the description.

air sacs	digestion	nutrients
calories	food groups	proteins
carbohydrates	kidneys	small intestine
diaphragm	lungs	urine

1. the process of breaking down food _____

2. organs that filter liquid waste _____

3. organs that take air into body _____

4. the muscle that moves the lungs _____

5. over 300 million of these make up the lungs _____

6. energy from food _____

7. tube that receives food from stomach _____

8. parts of food your body can use _____

9. found in the meat group and used for growth and repair _____

10. starches or sugars _____

11. four categories of food _____

12. liquid waste from the body _____

Part B

Eating foods from the four food groups will give you a balanced diet. Name the four food groups.

_____   _____

_____   _____

Fill in the circle in front of the word or phrase that best completes the sentence. The first one is done for you.

1. Your body's raw materials are
   ● nutrients.
   ⓑ cells.
   ⓒ bones.

2. Fats give your body
   ⓐ vitamins.
   ⓑ energy.
   ⓒ oxygen.

3. Citrus fruits have
   ⓐ vitamin A.
   ⓑ vitamin B.
   ⓒ vitamin C.

4. Cereals and breads are a
   ⓐ food group.
   ⓑ vitamin.
   ⓒ mineral.

5. Energy from food can be measured in
   ⓐ calories.
   ⓑ vitamins.
   ⓒ nutrients.

6. The unused part of food
   ⓐ stays in the heart.
   ⓑ is called waste.
   ⓒ goes into the lungs.

7. Carbohydrates are found in
   ⓐ grains.
   ⓑ water.
   ⓒ vitamins.

8. Fats are broken down by the
   ⓐ lungs.
   ⓑ liver.
   ⓒ mouth.

9. Urine moves from the kidneys to the
   ⓐ bladder.
   ⓑ large intestine.
   ⓒ rectum.

10. Keep your lungs healthy by
    ⓐ smoking.
    ⓑ exercising.
    ⓒ dieting.

Just for Fun

The sentences tell about some of your body systems. But one word in each sentence is scrambled. Unscramble the letters. Then write the correct word on the lines at the right. Choose from the words below. The first one is done for you.

bladder	kidneys	oxygen
dioxide	lungs	rectum
fat	mineral	vitamin

1. In order to live, cells constantly need ENXYGO.

   $\underline{O}$ $\underline{X}$ $\underline{Y}$ $\underline{G}$ $\underline{E}$ $\underline{N}$
                       1

2. The NGULS take air into the body.

   _ _ _ _ _
     2

3. The very last part of the digestive system is the UMCTER.

   _ _ _ _ _ _
       3

4. Iron is a ERINMAL needed by your body.

   _ _ _ _ _ _ _
         4

5. A waste gas produced by the body is called carbon DDEIXOI.

   _ _ _ _ _ _ _
     5

6. Urine passes from the kidneys to the DDELABR.

   _ _ _ _ _ _ _
          6

7. Citrus fruits are rich in INTAMVI C.

   _ _ _ _ _ _
          7

8. A nutrient found in butter is called TFA.

   _ _ _
     8

9. The two bean-shaped organs in your body are called NESYKID.

   _ _ _ _ _ _ _
          9

Solve the Secret Message. When a letter of a word above has a number under it, write that letter above the same number in the Secret Message.

Secret Message: What does your body use from the foods you eat?

_ _ _ _ _ _ _ _ _
1 2 3 4 5 6 7 8 9

UNIT 4 ▪ The Nervous System

What Does the Nervous System Do?

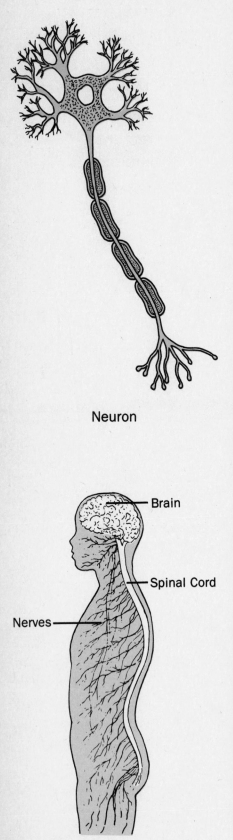

Neuron

Brain

Spinal Cord

Nerves

The Nervous System

The **nervous system** is like a computer for your body. It gets information from all parts of the body. It also gets information from the environment. It examines the information. Then it tells the body what to do. The nervous system does its job by carrying messages between the brain and spinal cord, and other parts of the body. The messages it carries are like tiny electric sparks.

The basic part of the nervous system is a cell called a **neuron**. Messages move from neuron to neuron along threadlike branches. The neurons are arranged in bundles called **nerves**.

Two main kinds of nerves are **sensory nerves** and **motor nerves**. Sensory nerves bring messages from the sense organs to the brain or the spinal cord. Your eyes, ears, nose, mouth, and skin are sense organs. Sense organs get information from the environment.

Motor nerves carry messages from the brain and the spinal cord to other parts of the body. How do these nerves work?

When you hear a friend say hello, sensory nerves carry the sound from your ears to your brain. Your brain understands the sound. It decides that you should wave.

The brain sends a message to the spinal cord. The spinal cord sends the message to motor nerves of your arm. These nerves cause the muscles of your arm to move. This action is voluntary. It is something you do on purpose. It happens because of a decision made by your brain.

A. Answer True or False.

1. The nervous system carries blood. _False_

2. The basic parts of the nervous system are neurons. _True_

3. Bundles of neurons are called electric sparks. _False_

4. Sense organs get information from the environment. _True_

5. Sensory nerves cause muscles to move. _False_

B. Fill in the missing word.

1. Sense organs get information from the _environment_.
   ((environment) muscles)

2. Bundles of neurons form _nerves_. (nerves, messages)

3. _Motor nerves_ can cause your muscles to move.
   ((Motor nerves) Sensory nerves)

4. Messages move from one _neuron_ to another along threadlike branches. (neuron, blood vessel)

C. Circle the letter of the correct answer.

1. Which gets information from the environment?
   (a) the skeletal system   (b) the nervous system   (c) the blood

2. Which carry messages from the sense organs to the brain or the spinal cord?
   (a) sensory nerves   (b) motor nerves   (c) blood vessels

3. Which cause muscles to move?
   (a) sensory nerves   (b) motor nerves   (c) blood vessels

D. Answer the question.

What does the nervous system do? _It gets information from all parts of the body. The nervous system does it's job by carrying messages between the brain & spinal cord and other parts of the body._

63

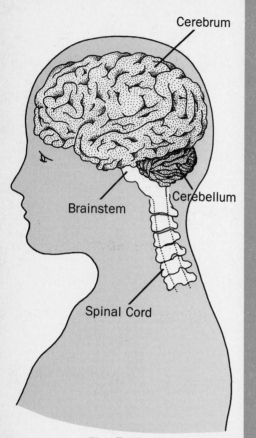

The Brain

(Labels on the diagram: Cerebrum, Cerebellum, Brainstem, Spinal Cord)

The main control center of the body is the brain. Together, the brain and the spinal cord direct all the actions of the body. The brain and the spinal cord make up the **central nervous system**.

Some of your actions involve your spinal cord but not your brain. Suppose you touch a hot pan. Sensory nerves in your skin send a message about heat to the spinal cord. The spinal cord sends the message to motor nerves. These nerves cause the muscles of your arm to move. The muscles pull your hand away from the pan before you get burned.

This action is a **reflex**. You do not have to use your brain to think about it. It is involuntary. Other reflexes are blinking, sneezing, and coughing.

Other kinds of actions are not as simple as reflexes. They involve different parts of the brain. Look at the drawing of the brain. Then look at the table. Find out which parts of the brain control different actions.

Part of the Brain	What It Controls
Cerebrum	Thinking, learning, speaking, writing, memory, voluntary muscle actions
Cerebellum	Balance for walking, running, and other motions like dancing
Brainstem	Breathing, swallowing, heartbeat, blood pressure, body temperature

A. **Answer True or False.**

1. A reflex is an involuntary action. __F__

2. Blinking and sneezing are reflexes. __T__

3. The brain is involved in every action of the body. __T__

4. The spinal cord is part of the nervous system. __F__

5. The brain controls reflex actions. __T__

B. **The steps of a reflex action are listed below. Number the steps in the correct order. The first one is done for you.**

__3__ Sensory nerves send a message of heat to the spinal cord.

__4__ You pull your hand away from the pan.

__5__ The spinal cord sends a message through the motor nerves.

__1__ You touch a hot pan.

__2__ Motor nerves cause the muscles of your arm to move.

C. **Use the table to answer the questions. Circle the letter of the correct answer.**

1. Which part of the brain controls learning?
   (a) cerebrum   (b) cerebellum   (c) brainstem

2. Which part of the brain controls breathing?
   (a) cerebrum   (b) cerebellum   (c) brainstem

3. Which part of the brain controls balance?
   (a) cerebrum   (b) cerebellum   (c) brainstem

D. **Answer the questions.**

1. What kind of action does __not__ use the brain? _____

   _____

2. What are two examples of reflex actions? _____

   _____

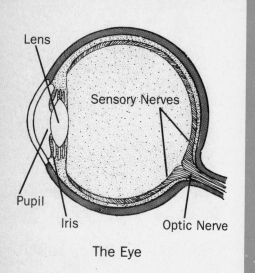

Lens

Sensory Nerves

Pupil

Iris

Optic Nerve

The Eye

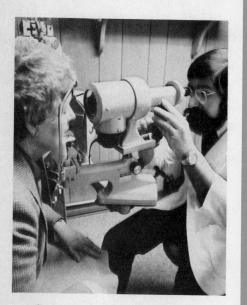

See an eye doctor once a year to have your eyes checked.

Your eyes are sense organs. Remember that sense organs send different kinds of messages to the brain and the spinal cord. Your eyes send pictures of the world to your brain.

The colored part of your eye is called the **iris**. Look at the drawing of the eye and its parts. The opening at the center of the iris is the **pupil**. If there isn't much light, the pupil opens to let in more light. This makes it easier to see in dim light. In bright light, the pupil gets smaller. This protects the eye from too much light.

The **lens** of the eye can focus light to make sharp pictures. It focuses light onto the back of the eyeball. Sensory nerves cover the back of the eyeball. These sensory nerves send pictures to the **optic nerve**. The optic nerve sends the pictures to the brain. The brain understands what you see.

Your eyes are protected in many ways. The cheek and forehead bones can protect your eyes from injury. Eyelashes catch dirt and dust before they can get into your eyes. By blinking, your eyelids spread tears over your eyes. Tears help keep your eyes moist and clean. Remember that blinking is a reflex action.

You can help take care of your eyes. Do not rub them. You may be rubbing dirt into your eyes. Keep sharp objects away from your eyes. Wear glasses if you need them. See an eye doctor once a year to have your eyes checked.

A. Fill in the missing word.

1. The eyes are one of the body's _motor nerves_.
   (sense organs, motor nerves)

2. The eye can send pictures to the _brain_. (brain, muscles)

3. The _lens_ focuses light on the back of the eyeball.
   (lens, optic nerve)

4. The _brain_ understands what the eye sees. (pupil, brain)

B. Circle the letter of the correct answer.

1. What is the opening called that lets light into the eye?
   (a) iris   (b) pupil   (c) lens ✓

2. Which part of the eye focuses light?
   (a) iris   (b) pupil   (c) lens ✓

3. Which part of the eye sends pictures to the optic nerve?
   (a) the pupil ✓   (b) sensory nerves   (c) the brain

4. What part of the eye sends pictures to the brain?
   (a) lens ✓   (b) the pupil   (c) optic nerve

C. Answer True or False.

1. Your eyes can send messages to the brain. _T_

2. If there is too much light, your pupils get larger. _F_

3. The lens of the eye can focus light to make pictures. _T_

4. Eyelashes help protect the eyes. _T_

D. Answer the question.

What three things can you do to protect your eyes? _Wear glasses if you need them._
Keep sharp objects away fro from youreye
Do not Rub them.

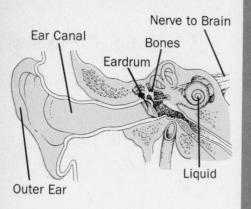

Ear Canal

Nerve to Brain

Bones

Eardrum

Outer Ear

Liquid

The Ear

You can lose your hearing by listening to very loud sounds or music.

When you speak, the air around you moves. This motion of the air is called a **vibration**. All sounds are the result of vibrations. How do you hear sounds?

Your ears are sense organs for hearing. As vibrations travel through the air, some are caught by the **outer ear**. This is the part of the ear that you can see. Then the vibrations pass down the **ear canal** to the inside of the ear.

The end of the canal is covered with a thin skin called the **eardrum**. When vibrations hit the eardrum, it vibrates. Then the vibrations are passed on to three tiny bones in the ear.

Next, the bones pass the vibrations on to a liquid inside the ear. Nerves are in contact with the liquid. These nerves send messages to the brain. The brain understands what the sounds mean.

Your ears also give you your sense of balance. Remember that nerves are in contact with the liquid in the ears. As you move, the liquid moves, too. Then the nerves send a message to the brain. Your brain understands that your head has changed position. This way you can keep your balance as you do things like ride a bicycle or walk.

You can take care of your ears. Keep your fingers and other objects out of them. Protect your ears from loud sounds. Objects and loud sounds can break an eardrum. If one of your eardrums breaks, you can lose most of the hearing in that ear.

A. Answer True or False.

1. The outer ear catches sound vibrations. _____

2. The eardrum sends messages to the brain. _____

3. There are no nerves in the ear. _____

4. Sounds are made by vibrations in the air. _____

5. You can safely put objects in your ears. _____

6. The outer ear passes vibrations on to the inside of the ear.

_____

B. Write the letter for the correct answer.

1. When sound vibrations hit it, the eardrum _____.
   (a) breaks   (b) vibrates   (c) shrinks

2. The eardrum passes vibrations on to the _____.
   (a) bones in the ear   (b) outer ear   (c) eye

3. The bones in the ear pass vibrations on to the _____.
   (a) liquid in the ear   (b) outer ear   (c) eardrum

4. Messages about sound are understood by the _____.
   (a) outer ear   (b) bones   (c) brain

C. The sentences below describe how you hear a sound. Number them in the correct order. The first one is done for you.

_____ The brain understands what the sound means.

___1___ The outside of the ear catches sound vibrations from the air.

_____ Bones pass vibrations on to a liquid inside the ear.

_____ The liquid vibrates.

_____ Nerves in contact with the liquid send a message to the brain.

_____ Vibrations are passed on to the eardrum.

_____ Vibrations from the eardrum are passed on to tiny bones.

Smell and Taste

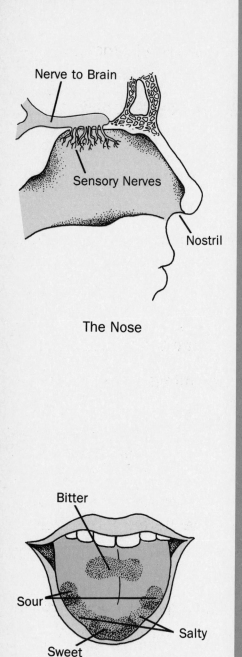

The Nose

Bitter

Sour

Sweet

Salty

The Tongue

Imagine going into a kitchen. Even without looking in the oven you know that bread is baking. How do you know that it is bread and not chicken, potatoes, or apple pie? Your sense of smell tells you. How does your nose work as a sense organ?

As you breathe in, you take in tiny particles of all the things around you. The sensory nerves in the nose respond to these particles. These sensory nerves send a message to the brain. The brain understands the message. It identifies the smell of bread. In fact, you can identify over 50 different smells.

Inside your mouth there are other sensory nerves. They bring messages to your brain about tastes. All these nerves are on the tongue. The nerves end in cells called **taste buds**. Taste buds can sense four flavors: sweet, sour, salty, and bitter. Not all taste buds sense the same flavor. Look at the drawing of the tongue. Where are the taste buds for salty foods?

Remember the last time you had a cold? How did your favorite food taste? It probably didn't have much of a taste at all. That is because your sense of smell and sense of taste work together. When you can't smell food, it may be hard to taste it.

Sometimes taste and smell can give you important information. Foods that have a bad smell may be spoiled. They may not be safe to eat. Some things that taste bitter may be poisonous.

70

A. Fill in the missing word.

1. The inside of the nose has _____ nerves. (optic, sensory)

2. The _____ can identify many different smells. (brain, spinal cord)

3. The ends of sensory nerves in the tongue are cells called _____. (particles, taste buds)

4. The four flavors that you can taste are sweet, _____, salty, and bitter. (sour, fresh)

5. You may not be able to taste food if you cannot _____ it. (smell, hear)

B. Answer True or False.

1. Sensory nerves in the nose send messages to the brain. _____

2. Sensory nerves in the mouth help you taste things. _____

3. Your tongue does not have any sensory nerves. _____

4. Sensory nerves in the tongue end in cells called taste buds.

   _____

5. Without your sense of smell, food would taste better. _____

C. Write the letter for the correct answer.

1. _____ in your nose send messages about smell to your brain.
   (a) Optic nerves   (b) Sensory nerves   (c) Taste buds

2. Sensory nerves in the tongue end in cells called _____.
   (a) motor nerves   (b) particles   (c) taste buds

3. Your senses of smell and _____ work together.
   (a) taste   (b) sight   (c) hearing

4. Taste buds can sense _____ flavors.
   (a) 25   (b) 12   (c) 4

5. Messages about both smell and taste go to the _____.
   (a) brain   (b) spinal cord   (c) eyes

71

Your sense of touch can identify different kinds of surfaces.

Your largest sense organ is your skin. The skin has many different layers. In the layers are sensory nerves. The nerves send messages to your brain about your sense of touch. Feel the top of your desk with the tip of your finger. Is the desk rough or smooth? Your brain gets a message when you touch something so you know how it feels.

There are more nerves for touch in your fingertips than in any other part of your body. Why would you need more nerves in your fingertips?

Nerves for touch are near the top of the skin. However, there are other nerves in deeper layers of the skin. Some of these nerves react to pressure. Push your hand against the edge of your desk. Feel the pressure in your hand. Other nerves react to heat and cold. Still others react to pain.

What happens if your hand touches a hot pan? Sensory nerves react to the heat. They send a message to the spinal cord. The spinal cord sends a message to the muscles of your arm. You pull your hand away from the heat. If you could not feel heat or pain, you could get easily burned or injured. The nerves of the skin protect you from this kind of injury.

Remember that the nerves of the skin send messages to the brain. The brain knows which nerve each kind of message comes from. So the brain knows the difference between a message for pain and one for touch.

A. Answer True or False.

1. There are many sensory nerves in the layers of the skin. _____

2. The fingertips have no sensory nerves for touch. _____

3. Sensory nerves in the skin cannot tell the difference between things that are rough and smooth. _____

4. Without the nerves of the skin, you might get injured. _____

B. Read each statement. Write yes in front of the things that the nerves in your skin can do. Write no in front of the things the nerves in your skin cannot do.

_____ 1. They can tell the difference between rough and smooth.

_____ 2. They can identify smells.

_____ 3. They can understand sounds.

_____ 4. They can react to pressure.

_____ 5. They can react to pain.

_____ 6. They can taste different foods.

_____ 7. They can react to heat.

_____ 8. They can react to cold.

C. Answer the questions.

1. What are three things that nerves in the skin react to? _____

_____

_____

2. What might happen to a person who did not have sensory nerves that react to heat? _____

3. How does the brain know the difference between pain and touch?

_____

_____

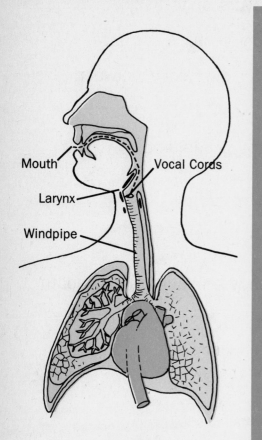

Mouth

Vocal Cords

Larynx

Windpipe

Think of all the sounds you can make. You can whisper or shout. You can talk in a deep voice or a high, squeaky voice. How can you make all these different sounds?

You use your mouth and the organs of the respiratory system to talk. First air is brought into your body. Then it is pushed out when you talk.

At the top of your windpipe is a voice box, or **larynx**. Inside the larynx are two folds of skin called the **vocal cords**. When air is pushed through the larynx, the vocal cords vibrate. These vibrations produce sounds. The sounds pass through the throat and out of the mouth. The harder you push the air through the vocal cords, the louder the sound.

Your vocal cords can make sounds that are high or low in pitch. That is because your vocal cords are controlled by muscles. When the muscles are stretched tight, your voice gets higher. When the muscles relax, your voice gets lower.

By moving your tongue and lips into different positions, you shape the sounds into words. Speak slowly while looking in a mirror. Try to see the positions of your tongue and lips as you say different words.

You need your tongue, lips, and respiratory system to talk. You also need your brain. Your brain sends messages to the vocal cords, tongue, and lips. These messages control what you say and how you say it.

A. Underline the answer to each question.

1. Which organ do you use for talking? (eyes, mouth)

2. What is another name for the voice box? (larynx, mouth)

3. What part of the mouth shapes sounds into words? (lips, windpipe)

4. Which is <u>not</u> needed for talking? (brain, heart)

5. What part vibrates when you talk? (teeth, vocal cords)

B. Write the letter for the correct answer.

1. You use both your mouth and your _____ to talk.
   (a) heart   (b) respiratory system   (c) digestive system

2. Your voice gets higher and lower because of your _____ .
   (a) vocal cords   (b) lips   (c) tongue

3. When air is forced through the larynx, the vocal cords _____ .
   (a) stop moving   (b) vibrate   (c) break

4. What you say and how you say it are controlled by your _____ .
   (a) brain   (b) lips   (c) lungs

C. Below is a list of steps that lead to talking. Number the steps in the correct order. The first one is done for you.

_____**1**_____ Air is brought into the body.

_____ Air is pushed through the larynx.

_____ Sounds pass out of the mouth and are changed into words.

_____ The vocal cords vibrate and produce sounds.

D. Answer the questions.

1. How do you make sounds louder when you talk? _____

_____

2. How are the sounds passing out of your mouth shaped into words?

_____

_____

Keeping the Nervous System Healthy

These foods help keep your nervous system healthy.

How can you keep your nervous system healthy? You can eat foods rich in proteins, calcium, and vitamin B. Meats, milk products, grains, and vegetables are sources of these nutrients.

Drinks such as coffee, tea, and some soft drinks contain **caffeine**. Caffeine can make your nervous system too active. You may feel jumpy or shaky. You may not be able to sleep.

Alcohol slows down the nervous system. People react slowly. They lose their sense of balance. Too much alcohol makes people unaware of what is going on around them. That is why it is so dangerous to drink alcohol and drive a car.

Think about what you put into your body. It can affect the way you think, feel, and act.

A. Answer True or False.

1. Foods with vitamin B help your nervous system. _____

2. Caffeine helps you sleep well. _____

3. Alcohol slows down the nervous system. _____

4. What you put into your body affects the way you feel. _____

B. Answer the questions.

1. What can caffeine do to the nervous system? _____

_____

2. What can alcohol do to the nervous system? _____

_____

Review

Part A

Complete each sentence. Use the words below.

brain	nervous system	sense organs
caffeine	optic nerve	vibrations
motor nerves	reflex	vocal cords

1. The _____ carries messages that are like tiny electric sparks.

2. Your ears and eyes are two of the _____ of your body.

3. Sneezing is an example of a _____.

4. Nerves that cause muscles to move are called _____.

5. Thinking and learning are controlled by the _____.

6. Drinks that contain _____ can make the nervous system too active.

7. Sounds that you hear are made by _____.

8. The nerve that sends pictures to the brain is the _____.

9. _____ make sounds that are high or low in pitch.

Part B

Draw a line to match the part of the sense organ with the job that the part does.

1. pupil   react to heat

2. vocal cords   catches vibrations in the air

3. taste buds   lets light into the eye

4. outer ear   vibrate to make sounds

5. nerves in the skin   sense flavors

Fill in the circle in front of the word or phrase that best completes each sentence. The first one is done for you.

1. Sending and receiving messages is the job of the
   - ● nervous system.
   - ⓑ heart.
   - ⓒ skeletal system.

2. A cell of the nervous system is called a
   - ⓐ neuron.
   - ⓑ eardrum.
   - ⓒ larynx.

3. Sensory nerves get messages from the
   - ⓐ brain.
   - ⓑ spinal cord.
   - ⓒ sense organs.

4. The sounds for talking are produced by
   - ⓐ vocal cords.
   - ⓑ taste buds.
   - ⓒ optic nerves.

5. Blinking and sneezing are
   - ⓐ voluntary actions.
   - ⓑ reflexes.
   - ⓒ thoughts.

6. In the eye, the optic nerve
   - ⓐ lets in light.
   - ⓑ identifies flavors.
   - ⓒ sends pictures to the brain.

7. When sound vibrations reach the eardrum, it
   - ⓐ swells.
   - ⓑ shrinks.
   - ⓒ vibrates.

8. Nerve cells on the tongue are called
   - ⓐ optic nerves.
   - ⓑ taste buds.
   - ⓒ vocal cords.

9. The largest sense organ is the
   - ⓐ brain.
   - ⓑ mouth.
   - ⓒ skin.

10. A drink that slows down the nervous system is
    - ⓐ alcohol.
    - ⓑ coffee.
    - ⓒ milk.

Each sentence below describes a part of the nervous system. Fill in the name of each part. Use the words below.

brain	nerves	spinal cord
coughing	nose	taste buds
eardrum	skin	tongue
ears		

1. This part helps change sounds into words.   _ _ _ _ _ _
                                                   2

2. This organ controls thinking.   _ _ _ _ _
                                       4

3. These are bundles of neurons.   _ _ _ _ _ _
                                         1

4. This is a reflex.   _ _ _ _ _ _ _ _
                        6

5. These organs pick up vibrations from the air.   _ _ _ _
                                                        8

6. This organ senses smell.   _ _ _ _
                                 7

7. This organ can sense cold.   _ _ _ _
                                 10

8. This part is involved in reflex actions.   _ _ _ _ _ _ _ _ _ _
                                                         5   3

9. This is the thin skin at the end of the ear canal.   _ _ _ _ _ _ _
                                                             9

Now solve the riddle. When a letter of a word above has a number under it, write that letter above the same number in the riddle.

Riddle: Singers love me. I can make their notes go high or low.

What am I? _ _ _ _ _ _ _ _ _ _
            1 2 3 4 5 6 7 8 9 10

UNIT 5 · Human Reproduction
Hormones and Glands

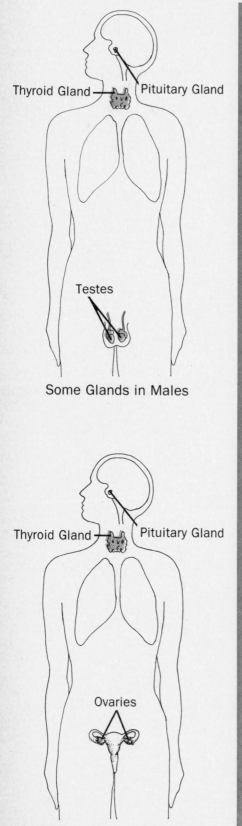

Thyroid Gland — Pituitary Gland

Testes

Some Glands in Males

Thyroid Gland — Pituitary Gland

Ovaries

Some Glands in Females

How tall are you going to get? How does your body stay warm? Why does a boy's voice change when he is 12 or 13?

All these activities are controlled by organs called **glands.** Your glands keep many body functions running smoothly.

Glands make special chemicals that bring messages to every part of your body. These chemical messengers are called **hormones.** Glands put hormones into the blood. Then the blood carries hormones to the parts of the body where they work.

The **pituitary gland** makes a hormone that is carried by the blood to the bones. This hormone makes the long bones of the skeleton grow. It helps you reach your adult size.

The **thyroid gland** controls how fast you use food and change it into energy. With too much of this hormone, the body releases a lot of energy. The heart speeds up. Body temperature goes up. The person may be nervous and lose weight.

Other glands make **sex hormones.** These hormones control the development of male and female sex characteristics. In girls, the sex glands are the **ovaries.** They make breasts develop and hips widen. In boys, the sex glands are the **testes.** They make the voice deepen and body hair grow.

In girls, changes in sex characteristics happen between 10 and 16 years of age. Boys change between 12 and 18. This time of change is called **puberty.** It is the stage between childhood and adulthood.

A. Complete the sentences. Use the words below.

| glands | ovaries | testes |
| hormones | puberty | thyroid |

1. Hormones are made in organs called _____.

2. Chemicals that bring messages to every part of the body are _____.

3. In boys, the sex glands are the _____.

4. In girls, the sex glands are the _____.

5. The stage between childhood and adulthood is called _____.

B. Answer True or False.

1. Hormones made in one part of the body can work in another part of the body. _____

2. Bones grow because of a hormone made in the pituitary gland. _____

3. Ovaries make body hair grow in boys. _____

4. Puberty is a kind of hormone. _____

C. Answer the questions.

1. What are the chemicals called that are made by glands? _____

2. What does the thyroid gland do? _____

3. What is puberty? _____

4. What makes the long bones of the skeleton grow? _____

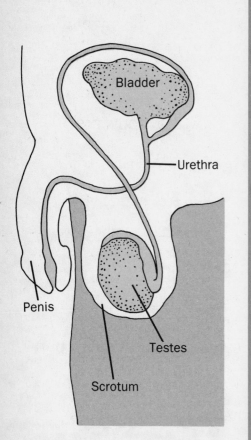

The Male Reproductive System

Bladder

Urethra

Penis

Testes

Scrotum

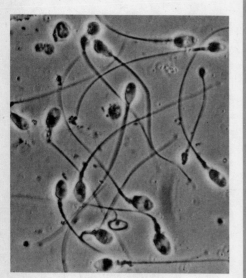

Sperm Cells

Boys have different sex organs than girls. In boys, the sex organs are two **testes.** The testes are on the outside of the male's body. They are in a sac of skin called the **scrotum.**

Sex organs work as glands. The testes make hormones. During puberty, they make a boy's body change to look more like a man's body. They are also important in reproduction. That's why sex organs are part of the **reproductive system.**

Testes make cells called **sperm.** Sperm are so small you need a microscope to see them. Males make sperm cells when they reach puberty. A male makes hundreds of millions of sperm in his lifetime.

Millions of sperm leave the testes and pass into a long, thin tube. There they are mixed with fluid to make **semen.** The semen passes into another tube under the bladder. This tube, the **urethra,** is in the **penis.** It leads semen out of the body.

A sperm cell must come together with an egg cell from a female for a baby to form. First, sperm is transferred into the female. Each sperm has a long, threadlike tail that moves back and forth and helps push the sperm along. The sperm must swim to the egg cell.

If a sperm meets an egg, they can join. This joining is called **fertilization.** Only one sperm cell can fertilize an egg cell.

The fertilized egg begins to grow. It grows and divides. It forms 2 cells. Then 2 cells divide and form 4 cells and so on. In about 9 months a baby is born. This is how a new human life begins.

A. Complete the sentences. Use the words below.

fertilization	scrotum	testes
penis	sperm cells	urethra

The male sex organs are called the _____. They are inside a sac of skin called the _____. The _____ are made in these organs. They leave the body through a tube called the _____ inside the _____. During _____, a sperm cell made in the male's sex organs joins with an egg cell from the female.

B. Write the letter for the correct answer.

1. The male reproductive system produces _____.
   (a) eggs   (b) sperm   (c) ovaries

2. Fertilization takes place inside the _____.
   (a) male   (b) female   (c) scrotum

3. A baby is made from _____.
   (a) a sperm only   (b) an egg only   (c) a sperm and an egg

C. Answer the questions.

1. What are two things that are made in the testes? _____

   _____

2. When do males start making sperm cells? _____

   _____

3. Why does a sperm cell need a tail? _____

   _____

4. What happens to an egg cell after it is fertilized? _____

   _____

   _____

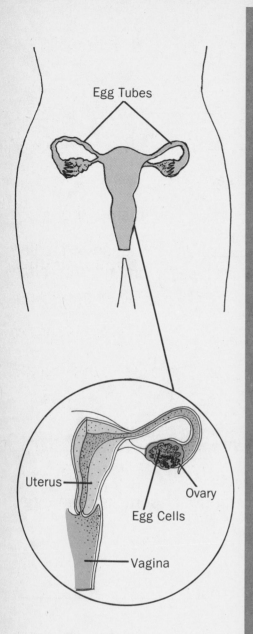

Egg Tubes

Uterus

Ovary

Egg Cells

Vagina

The Female Reproductive System

How are girls and boys different? Girls have sex organs called **ovaries.** Ovaries produce hormones that make a girl's body grow in different ways than a boy's body.

The two ovaries also store the cells that develop into babies. These cells are called **egg cells.** Females are born with all their eggs inside them. Then, when a girl gets old enough, one egg leaves one ovary every month. Where does the egg go?

The egg passes from the ovary into a tube. It takes about 3 days for the egg to travel down this tube to an organ called the **uterus.** By this time, tissues lining the uterus have filled with blood. They are ready to hold a developing baby.

If the egg cell is fertilized, it will stay in the uterus. It will develop into a **fetus.** The fetus will grow into a baby.

If the egg cell is not fertilized, the egg and the blood from the lining of the uterus are not needed. They leave the uterus and flow out of the body through the **vagina.** The vagina is also called the **birth canal,** because a baby passes through it when being born.

It takes about 5 days for the blood to flow out of the female's body. The female is having a **period.** The blood flow is part of the **menstrual cycle.** Things that happen again and again in the same order form a cycle. The menstrual cycle takes place about once a month.

Having a period is part of what makes girls and boys different. It is one of the changes in a girl's body. This change happens during puberty.

A. Answer True or False.

1. Girls have the same sex organs as boys. _____

2. Egg cells are needed for a fetus to develop. _____

3. Many egg cells leave an ovary every month. _____

4. A fetus can grow inside the uterus. _____

5. Ovaries produce hormones that make a girl's body different from a boy's body. _____

B. Fill in the missing words.

1. A fetus can grow in the _____. (ovaries, uterus)

2. The egg and the blood from the lining of the uterus flow out of the female's body through the _____. (vagina, ovaries)

3. The vagina is also called the _____. (uterus, birth canal)

4. A girl's body changes and she starts having a period _____. (when she is born, during puberty)

5. An egg passes from the ovary down a tube and into an organ called the _____. (uterus, testes)

C. Answer the questions.

1. What are a girl's sex organs called? _____

   _____

2. What kind of cell develops into a fetus? _____

   _____

3. Why do the tissues of the uterus fill with blood every month? _____

   _____

   _____

4. How often does the menstrual cycle take place? _____

   _____

Reproduction

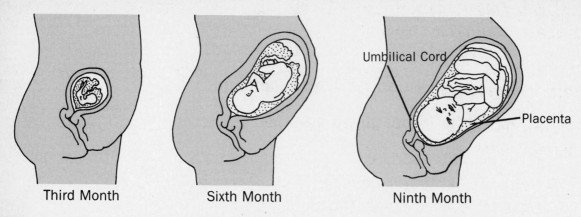

Umbilical Cord

Placenta

Third Month   Sixth Month   Ninth Month

The word **reproduce** means to make more. People reproduce by making babies.

You started life as one cell. This cell formed when sperm from your father fertilized an egg from your mother. Then you started to grow inside your mother. Your mother was **pregnant.** But how did you develop?

Blood vessels from the uterus and the developing fetus grow to form a tissue called the **placenta.** As more of the cells of the fetus grow, some of the cells form a tube. This tube is the **umbilical cord.** It attaches the fetus to the placenta.

When the mother eats, food is broken down into tiny particles. These particles flow through her blood to the placenta. Then they move through the umbilical cord and into the fetus. That's how the fetus gets food, oxygen, and water. Waste from the fetus passes into the mother through the placenta.

When a female is pregnant, she must rest and eat good food. She should not smoke or drink alcohol. These things can hurt the developing fetus.

After about 9 months the baby is ready to be born. The baby moves down through the birth canal and out the vagina. The doctor cuts the umbilical cord, which then becomes the baby's **navel.** The baby now breathes and eats outside its mother's body.

People belong to the group of animals called **mammals.** Female mammals have glands that make milk. Babies can use this milk as food.

A. Fill in the missing words.

1. A baby grows for about _____ before it is born.
   (1 year, 6 months, 9 months)

2. The placenta is made of _____.
   (a sperm cell, blood vessels, hair)

3. People belong to the group of animals called _____.
   (babies, mammals, males)

4. Food from the mother passes through the _____
   and into the fetus through the umbilical cord.
   (placenta, birth canal, mammal)

B. Answer True or False.

1. Smoking when pregnant is good for the developing fetus. _____

2. The baby leaves the mother's body through the vagina. _____

3. The umbilical cord is still needed after the baby is born. _____

4. Female mammals produce milk for their babies. _____

5. The developing fetus gets food on its own. _____

6. Waste passes from the fetus to the mother. _____

C. Answer the questions.

1. What does the word reproduce mean? _____

   _____

2. What does it mean when a woman is pregnant? _____

   _____

3. How does a developing fetus get food? _____

   _____

   _____

4. How does a developing fetus get rid of waste? _____

   _____

Getting Traits From Parents

Does the child look like her parents?

You might have the same color hair as your mother. Or you might be as tall as your father. Why do children look a lot like their parents?

You start life with one cell from your mother and one from your father. These cells have all the information you need to grow. This information is carried in parts of the cells called **chromosomes.**

Most cells have 46 chromosomes. You got 23 from your mother and 23 from your father. Chromosomes have smaller parts called **genes.**

Genes determine whether you will be a boy or a girl. They also determine your **traits.** Features like hair color and height are traits. The passing of traits from parents to children is called **heredity.**

Each person has a special set of traits. Only **identical twins** have exactly the same traits. Identical twins form when a fertilized egg divides into two parts. Each part develops into a baby.

A. Use each word to write a sentence about heredity.

1. traits _____

   _____

2. heredity _____

   _____

B. Answer True or False.

1. Genes decide things like hair color. _____

2. Only identical twins can have the same set of traits. _____

88

Review

Part A

After each sentence, write <u>True</u> if the sentence is true and <u>False</u> if the sentence is false.

1. The ovaries and testes are sex organs. _____

2. The thyroid gland controls how you change food into energy. _____

3. Heredity is the passing on of traits from parents to children. _____

4. The umbilical cord is found in the chromosomes. _____

5. Hormones that help develop male and female sex characteristics come from the pituitary gland. _____

6. Mammals have glands that produce milk. _____

7. The stage between childhood and adulthood is called pregnancy.

_____

Part B

Complete the sentences. Use the words below.

fertilization	placenta	sperm
period	pregnant	umbilical cord

1. _____ combine with fluid to make semen.

2. The flow of blood in the menstrual cycle is called a _____.

3. Before an egg cell can grow into a fetus, _____ must take place.

4. The _____ is a tube that attaches a fetus to the placenta.

5. Blood vessels from the uterus and the developing fetus form a tissue called

   the _____.

Fill in the circle in front of the word or phrase that best completes the sentence. The first one is done for you.

1. Chemical messengers are
   ⓐ glands.
   ● hormones.
   ⓒ egg cells.

2. Food passes to the fetus through the
   ⓐ pituitary.
   ⓑ thyroid.
   ⓒ placenta.

3. The joining of egg and sperm is
   ⓐ puberty.
   ⓑ fertilization.
   ⓒ heredity.

4. Traits are carried by
   ⓐ genes.
   ⓑ blood vessels.
   ⓒ hormones.

5. Passing on of traits is
   ⓐ puberty.
   ⓑ hormones.
   ⓒ heredity.

6. Reproduce means to
   ⓐ grow body hair.
   ⓑ make more.
   ⓒ make hormones.

7. The male sex organs are called the
   ⓐ sperm cells.
   ⓑ testes.
   ⓒ ovaries.

8. The menstrual cycle takes place
   ⓐ once a month.
   ⓑ once a year.
   ⓒ once in a lifetime.

9. The female sex organs are called the
   ⓐ ovaries.
   ⓑ birth canal.
   ⓒ placenta.

10. A baby is born through the
    ⓐ placenta.
    ⓑ testes.
    ⓒ vagina.

Just for Fun

Use the clues to complete the puzzle. Choose from the words below.

eggs	ovaries	reproduce
genes	placenta	sperm
glands	puberty	testes
hormones		

Across

2. to make more
3. they carry traits
4. food moves from here to the umbilical cord
5. stored in ovaries
6. male sex organs
8. female sex organs

Down

1. chemical messengers
3. organs that make hormones
4. stage between childhood and adulthood
7. swims to reach the egg cell

Diseases Caused by Bacteria

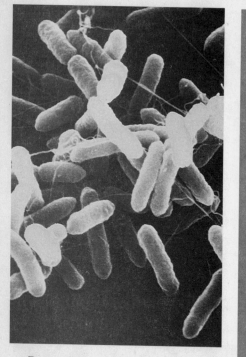

Bacteria can be seen with a microscope.

Many people are healthy most of their lives. But sometimes a person can become ill with a **disease.** Then some part of the body may not work properly.

Some diseases are caused by **bacteria.** Bacteria are tiny one-celled living things. Some are so small that a million could fit on the head of a pin. Bacteria can reproduce very quickly. Some bacteria can multiply every 20 minutes.

Bacteria cause disease in two ways. Some destroy body cells by feeding on them. Others make poisons, or **toxins,** that harm people.

Many diseases of the respiratory system are caused by bacteria. Remember that the respiratory system brings oxygen into the body. One of these diseases is **pneumonia.** Pneumonia is a serious infection of the lungs. People with pneumonia have chills and fever. They have a cough and chest pains.

Another disease caused by bacteria is **whooping cough.** Whooping cough is more common in children than adults. People with this disease cannot breathe easily. They have a cough and a fever.

Both pneumonia and whooping cough can be spread from one person to another. This happens when an infected person coughs. The cough sends a watery spray into the air. The spray carries the bacteria that cause the disease. Other people can breathe in these bacteria. Then they may become ill, too.

A. Answer True or False.

1. When a person has a disease, some part of the body does not work properly. _____

2. Some diseases are caused by bacteria. _____

3. Bacteria are tiny one-celled living things. _____

4. Bacteria can reproduce quickly. _____

5. Bacteria never harm a person's body cells. _____

6. Certain bacteria can cause pneumonia. _____

7. Pneumonia cannot be spread to other people. _____

B. Fill in the missing word.

1. Some bacteria make poisons called _____. (toxins, cells)

2. Bacteria are _____. (plants, cells)

3. Bacteria can cause diseases of the _____ system. (respiratory, skeletal)

4. Some bacteria can cause disease by feeding on body _____. (toxins, cells)

C. Answer the questions.

1. What are two diseases that are caused by bacteria? _____

   _____

2. What are two ways that bacteria can cause disease? _____

   _____

   _____

3. How can a disease like pneumonia be spread from one person to another?

   _____

   _____

   _____

Diseases Caused by Viruses

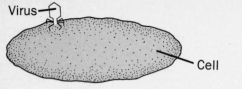

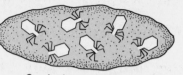

1. A virus enters a cell.

2. A virus reproduces inside the cell.

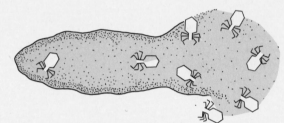

3. Many virus particles burst out of the cell.

Almost everyone has had a **cold** or the **flu.** These diseases are caused by **viruses.** Viruses are not cells. They are very tiny particles. Some viruses are a hundred times smaller than bacteria.

There are many kinds of viruses. All of them cause disease. A virus causes a disease by getting inside a body cell. The virus takes over the cell. It changes the way the cell works. It uses the cell's food.

The virus can reproduce inside the cell. Many virus particles are made. Soon the cell bursts open and all the virus particles pour out. Then they take over other healthy cells.

Besides colds and the flu, viruses can cause other diseases. **Measles, chicken pox,** and **mumps** are three other diseases caused by viruses.

Diseases caused by viruses can be spread from one person to another. When a person with a cold or the flu coughs or sneezes, virus particles go into the air. People can breathe the air carrying the virus particles. Then they can get sick, too. Measles and chicken pox can also be spread in this way.

You can also get measles by using the towels, dishes, or other objects used by an infected person. Chicken pox can be spread in this way, too.

A. Answer True or False.

1. Viruses are smaller than bacteria. _____

2. Colds and flu are caused by bacteria. _____

3. Viruses reproduce inside body cells. _____

4. Diseases caused by viruses can spread from one person to another. _____

B. Write the letter for the correct answer.

1. Colds are caused by _____.
   (a) bacteria   (b) viruses   (c) body cells

2. Viruses are _____.
   (a) tiny particles   (b) small cells   (c) large cells

3. Viruses cause measles, chicken pox, and _____.
   (a) mumps   (b) whooping cough   (c) bacteria

4. To cause a disease, a virus must _____.
   (a) get into a body cell   (b) be large   (c) be healthy

C. Answer the questions.

1. What are three diseases caused by viruses? _____

   _____

   _____

2. Where can a virus reproduce? _____

   _____

3. How does a virus spread from one body cell to another? _____

   _____

4. What is one way that measles can be spread from one person to another?

   _____

   _____

Body Defenses

Skin and Mucus

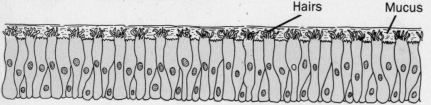

Hairs   Mucus

Hairs and mucus in your nose and throat are part of the body's defense against germs.

There are bacteria and viruses all around you. Yet you are healthy most of the time. This is true because your body has ways to protect you.

The body's first line of defense is the skin. The skin keeps bacteria and viruses from getting into the body. If you cut your skin, then bacteria and viruses can get into the body through the cut.

Bacteria or viruses can get into your body when you breathe. Your body has another way to defend you. Your nose and throat are lined with tissues that make a liquid called **mucus**. The sticky mucus traps many bacteria and viruses. They leave the body in a cough or a sneeze.

The tissues in the nose and throat also have tiny hairs. The hairs sweep mucus and particles up toward the mouth. Then they are swallowed and do not harm the body.

A. Answer True or False.

1. Bacteria and viruses can get into the body through a cut in the skin. _____

2. The body can't defend itself from bacteria or viruses that get in through the nose. _____

B. Answer the question.

How does your skin protect you from disease? _____

_____

Body Defenses

White Blood Cells

Suppose you cut your hand. Bacteria get into your body through the cut. But your body can still defend itself. It can use its white blood cells.

White blood cells are in your blood. They are always moving through your body. When you are cut, more white blood cells move to the area. They destroy bacteria.

When the white blood cells destroy the bacteria, the skin around the cut gets red. It swells up. There may be **pus** in the cut. Pus is made of dead bacteria and white blood cells. It is a sign that the white blood cells are working.

If you do cut yourself, try to keep bacteria from getting into your body. Wash the area around the cut to get rid of the bacteria on your skin. See a doctor if the cut is deep.

Washing your skin will get rid of bacteria that could enter a cut.

A. The steps below describe what happens when bacteria get into your body. Put the steps in order. The first one is done for you.

_____ Bacteria get into the body through the cut.

_____ Pus may form in the cut.

____1____ The skin is cut.

_____ White blood cells move to the cut.

_____ White blood cells destroy the bacteria.

B. Answer the question.

How do white blood cells help keep you healthy? _____

Body Defenses

Antibodies

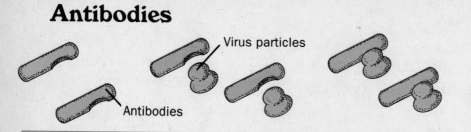

Virus particles

Antibodies

An antibody attaches to a virus and destroys it.

What happens if bacteria enter your skin through a cut? White blood cells destroy the bacteria. But many **germs** can enter your body. They can get into your cells and start to reproduce. The white blood cells may not be enough to destroy them.

Your body has another way to defend itself. It makes chemicals called **antibodies**. A special antibody is made for each kind of germ that attacks you.

Suppose the virus that causes measles gets into your body. If you have never had measles before, you will get sick. But your body makes antibodies that attack the measles virus. You get better. Some of the antibodies stay in your blood.

The measles virus might get into your body again. But your body already has antibodies to attack the virus. It quickly makes more. The virus is destroyed. You do not get measles a second time.

A. Answer <u>True</u> or <u>False</u>.

1. A special antibody is made for each kind of germ. _____

2. An antibody is a red blood cell. _____

B. Use each word in a sentence about body defenses.

1. antibodies _____

_____

2. measles _____

_____

Vaccines

When you were very young, you went to the doctor a number of times. Each time you got a shot, or an **injection**. These shots were **vaccines**. Vaccines help your body protect itself from diseases like whooping cough, measles, and mumps.

How do vaccines work? Vaccines are made of bacteria or virus particles that are weak or dead. The bacteria or viruses are not strong enough to make you sick. But the body still recognizes them as germs that can cause disease. So the body thinks that it is being attacked. It makes antibodies against the bacteria or virus.

Then when you come in contact with the bacteria or the virus, you will not get sick. The antibodies made in your body will destroy the bacteria or virus.

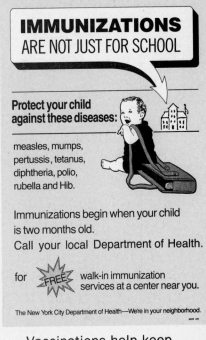

IMMUNIZATIONS ARE NOT JUST FOR SCHOOL

Protect your child against these diseases:

measles, mumps, pertussis, tetanus, diphtheria, polio, rubella and Hib.

Immunizations begin when your child is two months old.
Call your local Department of Health.

for FREE walk-in immunization services at a center near you.

The New York City Department of Health—We're in your neighborhood.

Vaccinations help keep diseases from spreading.

A. Answer <u>True</u> or <u>False</u>.

1. You can get a disease from taking a vaccine. _____

2. Vaccines are made of dead white blood cells. _____

B. Answer the questions.

1. Why don't the bacteria or viruses in vaccines make you sick?

_____

_____

2. Suppose you get the vaccine against measles. Will you get sick when you are in contact with the measles virus? Why or why not?

_____

_____

AIDS

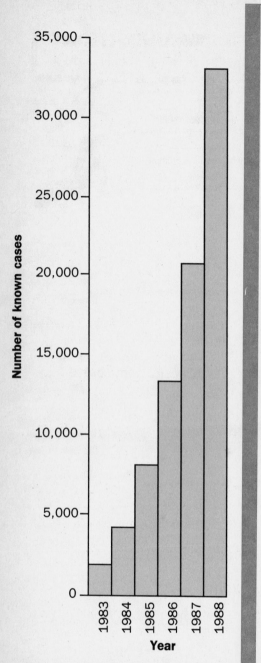

AIDS Cases in the United States

White blood cells are an important part of the system that keeps you healthy. Your body can defend itself when germs attack by sending white blood cells to destroy the germs.

But there is a virus that destroys white blood cells. This virus causes a condition called **AIDS**. People with AIDS are not protected from other diseases. They can get a rare kind of pneumonia. They can also get a rare kind of cancer. Pneumonia and cancer are the leading causes of death in AIDS patients.

The AIDS virus can be spread from one person to another. It can be spread when a person has sexual contact with a person who has AIDS. AIDS can also be spread by coming in contact with the blood of an infected person. Drug users who share needles with infected people can get AIDS. A pregnant woman with AIDS can give the virus to her baby.

AIDS cannot be spread by touching an infected person. It is not spread through the air, as colds or the flu are. Touching things used by a person with AIDS does not spread the virus.

So far, there is no cure for AIDS. Some drugs can help people with AIDS live longer. More drugs are being tested. Scientists are also trying to make a vaccine against the AIDS virus. Then people would have the antibodies to be protected from getting AIDS.

The graph on this page shows the number of known cases of AIDS in the United States. How has the number changed since 1983?

100

A. Answer True or False.

1. AIDS is caused by a virus. _____

2. The virus that causes AIDS destroys red blood cells. _____

3. People with AIDS cannot get other diseases. _____

4. Scientists are trying to find a vaccine for AIDS. _____

5. There is a cure for AIDS. _____

6. AIDS can be spread by touching a person who has the disease. _____

B. Fill in the missing words.

1. The virus that causes AIDS destroys _____. (red blood cells, white blood cells)

2. People with AIDS often get pneumonia or _____. (cancer, colds)

3. AIDS _____ be spread through the air, as colds are. (can, cannot)

4. AIDS can be spread by coming into contact with the _____ of an infected person. (blood, dishes)

5. Some drugs can help people with AIDS to _____. (live longer, get cancer)

C. Answer the questions.

1. What are the leading causes of death in AIDS patients? _____

_____

2. What are two ways that AIDS can be spread? _____

_____

_____

3. What are scientists doing to fight AIDS? _____

_____

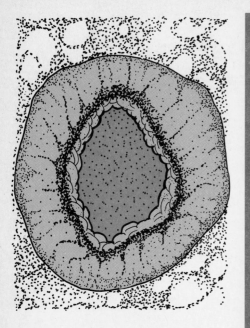

Normal Artery

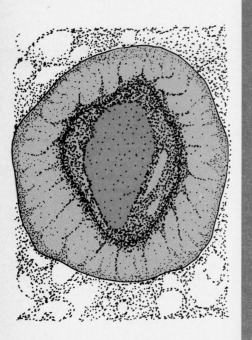

Artery Blocked with Cholesterol

Remember that some diseases are caused by bacteria and viruses. These diseases can be spread from one person to another. But people can get sick in other ways. They can get **disorders**. A disorder is a disease that lasts a long time or that gets worse in time. Disorders can't be spread to other people.

Heart diseases are some of the most common disorders. Each year, more people die from heart disease than any other disease.

One of the main heart diseases is high blood pressure. When the heart pumps blood, the blood pushes against the walls of the blood vessels. This push is blood pressure. High blood pressure occurs when the blood vessels are narrower than normal. Then the heart has to work harder to move the blood.

High blood pressure can lead to a **stroke**. In a stroke, a blood vessel breaks. Blood does not get to the brain. Nerve cells in the brain die. The person may not be able to speak or to move parts of his/her body. If many nerve cells die, the person dies.

In another kind of heart disease, the arteries can be blocked by a fat called **cholesterol**. This may lead to a heart attack. A **heart attack** causes parts of the heart to die because less blood gets to the heart. If the amount of damage is small, the person can get well. If a large part of the heart is damaged, the person may die.

A. Write the letter for the correct answer.

1. Disorders are diseases that _____ .
   (a) can be spread easily   (b) last a long time
   (c) are caused by viruses and bacteria

2. One of the main heart diseases is _____ .
   (a) low blood pressure   (b) high blood pressure
   (c) pneumonia

3. In a heart attack, parts of the heart _____ .
   (a) grow   (b) get strong   (c) die

4. High blood pressure can lead to _____ .
   (a) a stroke   (b) measles   (c) weight gain

B. Use each word in a sentence about heart disease.

1. cholesterol _____

   _____

2. high blood pressure _____

   _____

3. disorders _____

   _____

C. Answer the questions.

1. What is a disorder? _____

   _____

2. How is a disorder different from a disease caused by a virus? ____

   _____

3. What are some of the most common disorders? _____

   _____

4. How does cholesterol cause a heart attack? _____

   _____

   _____

Cancer

PLANNING A HEALTHY DIET
1. Cut down on fats. Eat more chicken and fish, and less beef.
2. Eat more carbohydrates, like bran cereals, baked potatoes, and fresh fruit.
3. Eat foods rich in vitamins A and C, like carrots, broccoli, and cirtrus fruits.
4. Eat fewer smoked or cured meats, like bacon, ham, or sausage.

Cancer is another kind of disorder. With cancer, body cells grow and multiply much faster than normal. The cancer cells can form a mass called a **tumor**. The cells of a tumor use the food needed for normal cells. They can also move to other parts of the body and grow.

No one knows for sure what causes cancer. Also, different kinds of cancers may have different causes.

Some things make cancers more likely to develop. Smoking, for example, can lead to lung cancer. More people in the United States have lung cancer than any other kind of cancer.

Getting too much sun can lead to skin cancer. People who have light skin are at greater risk. They should protect themselves with special creams that block the sun.

Only heart diseases kill more people in the United States than cancer. But many kinds of cancer can be treated. Some tumors can be removed from the body. Patients can be given chemicals that kill fast-growing cancer cells. Patients can also be treated with **radiation**. Radiation is a kind of energy that can destroy cancer cells.

People can also protect themselves. They can stop smoking. They can protect themselves from the sun. A good diet may also help to lower a person's chances of getting some kinds of cancer. Look at the table on this page. It shows some ways to plan a healthy diet.

A. Answer True or False.

1. In cancer, body cells multiply very fast. _____

2. A mass of cancer cells forms a tumor. _____

3. Lung cancer is caused by too much sunlight. _____

4. Cancer causes more deaths than heart disease. _____

5. A healthy diet can lower your chances of getting some kinds of cancer. _____

6. Chemicals and radiation can kill cancer cells. _____

7. Tumors cannot be removed from the body. _____

B. Use the table to answer the question.

What are two foods that should be a part of a healthy diet? _____

_____

_____

C. Answer the questions.

1. How are cancer cells different from normal cells? _____

_____

_____

2. Smoking can lead to what kind of cancer? _____

_____

3. Which disorder causes more deaths than cancer? _____

_____

4. What are three ways people can protect themselves from getting cancer?

_____

_____

_____

_____

Preventing Disease

SOME WAYS TO STAY HEALTHY
1. Eat a balanced diet.
2. Get about 8 hours of sleep every night.
3. Exercise for about 20 minutes 3 times a week.
4. Wash your hands before you eat and after going to the bathroom.
5. Bathe or shower often.
6. Do not use the dishes, glasses, towels, or other objects of a person with a cold or the flu.
7. Get regular checkups from a doctor.

How can you keep from getting diseases caused by bacteria or viruses? You can start by taking care of your body. If you are tired or do not eat well, your body defenses will not work at their best. Look at the table on this page for some ways to stay healthy.

Suppose you get a cold or the flu. Try not to spread it to others. Stay at home for a day or two so other people do not catch your cold. Cover your nose and mouth when you cough or sneeze.

People can also lower their chances of getting disorders like heart disease. They can eat a balanced diet that is low in fats. They can exercise. Exercise helps keep heart muscles strong. It also helps a person lose weight. People who are overweight have a greater chance of getting heart disease.

Regular visits to a doctor are important, too. In these checkups, a doctor can find high blood pressure and other signs of heart disease. A doctor can also find early signs of cancer.

Answer True or False.

1. Your body defenses work best when you are tired. _____

2. You can't lower your chances of getting heart disease. _____

3. Exercise helps keep heart muscle strong. _____

4. During a checkup, a doctor can find early signs of cancer. _____

5. You should cover your nose and mouth when you sneeze or cough.

_____

■ Review

Part A

Read each sentence. Write <u>True</u> if the sentence is true and <u>False</u> if it is false.

1. Bacteria are tiny one-celled living things. _____

2. Viruses are larger than bacteria. _____

3. Some diseases are caused by bacteria. _____

4. Pneumonia is a disease caused by bacteria. _____

5. All viruses cause disease. _____

6. Viruses reproduce only in water. _____

7. Measles are caused by bacteria. _____

8. Sneezing can spread a cold or the flu. _____

9. Heart diseases are not common disorders. _____

10. Cancer cells multiply faster than normal cells. _____

11. AIDS is caused by a virus that destroys white blood cells. _____

12. You cannot protect yourself from getting diseases. _____

13. A diet low in fats helps prevent heart disease. _____

Part B

Match each description with a word below.

antibodies	skin	tumor	vaccine

1. This part of the body keeps out bacteria and viruses. _____

2. This is a mass of cancer cells. _____

3. These chemicals kill germs that attack you. _____

4. This shot causes the body to make antibodies. _____

Fill in the circle in front of the word or phrase that best completes the sentence. The first one is done for you.

1. Bacteria can cause
   - ⓐ cancer.
   - ● pneumonia.
   - ⓒ mumps.

2. Colds are caused by
   - ⓐ disorders.
   - ⓑ viruses.
   - ⓒ cancer.

3. Diseases caused by bacteria and viruses can be spread by
   - ⓐ resting.
   - ⓑ sneezing and coughing.
   - ⓒ reading.

4. The part of the body that keeps out germs is the
   - ⓐ skin.
   - ⓑ lungs.
   - ⓒ brain.

5. To destroy germs, your body makes chemicals called
   - ⓐ measles.
   - ⓑ viruses.
   - ⓒ antibodies.

6. White blood cells can destroy
   - ⓐ antibodies.
   - ⓑ bacteria.
   - ⓒ red blood cells.

7. Vaccines cause the body to
   - ⓐ get sick.
   - ⓑ make viruses.
   - ⓒ make antibodies.

8. High blood pressure can cause
   - ⓐ a stroke.
   - ⓑ cancer.
   - ⓒ the flu.

9. Cancer cells
   - ⓐ are like normal cells.
   - ⓑ grow very slowly.
   - ⓒ grow very quickly.

10. Your body defenses work best when you are
   - ⓐ healthy.
   - ⓑ tired.
   - ⓒ sneezing.

Just for Fun

The questions below are about diseases. Use the words below to answer each question. Write the answers in the spaces at the right.

antibodies	exercise	toxin
body cells	heart diseases	vaccine
cholesterol	measles	

1. What are some of the most common disorders?   ◯___ ___ ___   ___ ___ ___ ___ ___ ___

2. What activity can keep your heart muscles strong?   ___ ___ ___ ___ ___ ___ ___◯

3. What chemicals are made by your body to attack germs?   ◯___ ___ ___ ___ ___ ___ ___ ___ ___

4. Which disease is caused by a virus?   ___ ___ ___ ___◯___ ___

5. What is the poison that some bacteria make?   ◯___ ___ ___ ___

6. What kind of fat can block arteries?   ___◯___ ___ ___ ___ ___ ___ ___ ___ ___

7. Where can a virus reproduce?   ___ ___ ___◯ ___ ___ ___ ___ ___

Write the circled letters on the numbered lines below. Then read the Secret Message.

Secret Message: You learn about diseases so you can find out

how to stay ___ ___ ___ ___ ___ ___ ___.
                  1   2   3   4   5   6   7

109

Health and Smoking

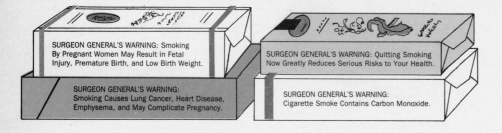

SURGEON GENERAL'S WARNING: Smoking By Pregnant Women May Result in Fetal Injury, Premature Birth, and Low Birth Weight.

SURGEON GENERAL'S WARNING: Quitting Smoking Now Greatly Reduces Serious Risks to Your Health.

SURGEON GENERAL'S WARNING: Smoking Causes Lung Cancer, Heart Disease, Emphysema, and May Complicate Pregnancy.

SURGEON GENERAL'S WARNING: Cigarette Smoke Contains Carbon Monoxide.

By law, all cigarette packs must have one of these messages.

Every day, 50 million Americans use **tobacco.** Some people chew it in the form of chewing tobacco. A few inhale it as a powder known as snuff. But most people smoke tobacco in cigarettes, cigars, and pipes.

Smoking became common hundreds of years ago. At that time, people did not know that the smoking habit could harm their health. But today, people have a lot of information about the effects of smoking. They know that smoking can increase the heartbeat. It can produce a bad cough or make breathing difficult. Smoking destroys vitamins in the body. It even harms people who breathe in the smoke from another person's cigarette.

People are also given warnings about the more serious effects of smoking. Smoking can lead to diseases of the circulatory system and the respiratory system. Every year, about 350,000 people in the United States die from diseases related to smoking. If people know about these effects, why do they smoke?

People smoke for many reasons. Ads in newspapers and magazines show smokers as healthy people having fun. Young people may start to smoke because they think it makes them look older. They may also smoke because their friends smoke.

Yet more and more people today are listening to the warnings. They want to stay healthy. One of the ways to stay healthy is to choose not to smoke.

A. Answer True or False.

1. Smoking can slow down the heartbeat. _____

2. Smoking can lead to diseases of the respiratory system. _____

3. People who do not smoke cannot be harmed by tobacco smoke. _____

4. People have a lot of information about the harmful effects of smoking. _____

B. Fill in the missing words.

1. Hundreds of years ago, people did not know that smoking could _____ their health. (harm, help)

2. Smoking can make breathing _____. (easy, difficult)

3. Young people may start to smoke because they think smoking makes them _____. (look older, healthy)

4. Smoking can lead to _____ of the circulatory system and the respiratory system. (diseases, health)

5. Ads in newspapers and magazines show smokers as _____ people. (sick, healthy)

C. Answer the questions.

1. What are three effects that smoking has on the body? _____

_____

_____

_____

_____

2. What is one reason why young people start to smoke? _____

_____

_____

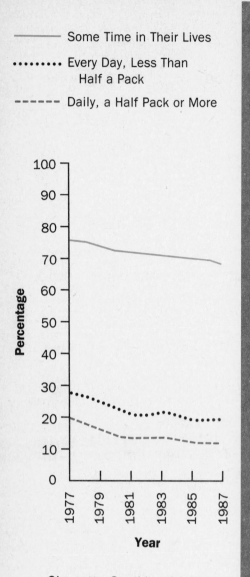

Some Time in Their Lives

Every Day, Less Than Half a Pack

Daily, a Half Pack or More

Cigarette Smoking Among
High School Seniors

Tobacco has many substances that can harm the body. The 3 most dangerous substances are **nicotine, tar,** and **carbon monoxide.**

When tobacco is smoked, the smoker inhales nicotine. Nicotine has harmful effects on the body. It can make the heart beat faster. It can raise blood pressure. Also, nicotine is an **addictive drug.** After getting used to an addictive drug, the body wants it all the time. It is very difficult to break nicotine addiction, even for smokers who want to stop smoking.

About 30 percent of tobacco smoke is made up of tar. Tar is a dark, sticky mixture of many chemicals. Tar can damage cells in the respiratory system. Then germs that cause disease are able to enter the lungs. The chemicals in tar can also lead to cancer of the mouth, throat, and lungs.

Burning tobacco also gives off carbon monoxide. This is the same poisonous gas given off by cars. Whether carbon monoxide is inhaled from cigarettes or from cars, it causes less oxygen to be carried by the blood through the body.

Nicotine, tars, and carbon monoxide can lead to diseases of the respiratory system and the circulatory system. These substances can affect people who do not smoke, as well as smokers. People who do not smoke are more likely to get these diseases if they breathe in tobacco smoke from the air. Today, many public places are divided into smoking and no-smoking areas. In this way, people who don't smoke can stay away from harmful tobacco smoke.

A. Fill in the missing words.

1. The three most dangerous substances in tobacco are tar, carbon monoxide, and _____. (air, nicotine)

2. Nicotine can make the heart beat faster and raise _____. (body temperature, blood pressure)

3. Some of the chemicals in tar can lead to _____. (cancer, high blood pressure)

4. Burning tobacco gives off _____ gas. (oxygen, carbon monoxide)

5. People who breathe in tobacco smoke are more likely to _____. (stay healthy, get diseases)

B. Answer True or False.

1. Smoking can lead to diseases of the respiratory system and the circulatory system. _____

2. Carbon monoxide is given off by burning tobacco and by cars. _____

3. People who do not smoke are not harmed by tobacco smoke in the air. _____

4. Nicotine, tar, and carbon monoxide can affect smokers and people who do not smoke. _____

C. Answer the questions.

1. What are the three most dangerous substances in tobacco smoke?

_____

_____

2. What happens when the body gets used to an addictive drug? _____

_____

113

Health and Alcohol

Beer: 12 ounces

Wine: 5 ounces

Whiskey: 1.5 ounces

Each drink has about the same amount of alcohol.

Drinks such as beer, wine, and whiskey have alcohol in them. Drinking alcohol can harm the body.

Why do you think people drink alcohol? Alcohol can make people feel good for a while. Cares and worries seem to go away. People feel more relaxed. People often have alcohol at parties. After a drink, people may find it easier to talk.

But these effects come from drinking small amounts of alcohol. Look at the picture on this page. It shows how beer, wine, and whiskey compare in amounts of alcohol. For most people, alcohol in small amounts is not a big problem. For some people, small amounts are not enough. They drink in large amounts. These people are doing great harm to their bodies.

People who drink a lot for a long time can have problems with their health. These people are abusing alcohol. To **abuse** something is to use it the wrong way or to use it too much.

Alcohol abuse can lead to diseases of the liver and the heart. It can also lead to a very serious addiction called **alcoholism.**

People who cannot stop abusing alcohol are called alcoholics. Most alcoholics know they have a serious problem. They can get help by going to one of the many groups that help alcoholics while they are getting over their addiction.

There are also special groups for the families of alcoholics. These groups help people deal with the problems caused by an alcoholic in the family.

A. Answer True or False.

1. Unlike smoking tobacco, drinking alcohol cannot harm the body.

   _____

2. Drinking alcohol can make people feel good for a while. _____

3. Drinking alcohol in small or large amounts is the same. _____

4. For most people, alcohol in large amounts is not harmful. _____

5. People who drink a lot for a long time are abusing alcohol. _____

6. Alcohol abuse can lead to diseases of the body. _____

B. Fill in the missing word or words.

1. Beer, wine, and whiskey all have _____ in them. (fruit, alcohol)

2. Alcohol abuse can lead to _____ and heart disease. (liver, lung)

3. Alcohol abuse may lead to a serious addiction called

   _____. (alcoholism, light drinking)

4. Drinking large amounts of alcohol can _____ the body. (harm, help)

C. Circle the letter of the correct answer.

1. The drink that does not contain alcohol is

   (a) beer.   (b) wine.   (c) apple juice.

2. Look at the picture on page 114. When glasses of beer, wine, and whiskey have the same amount of alcohol, the biggest drink is

   (a) beer.   (b) wine.   (c) whiskey.

3. Liver and heart disease may come from

   (a) one drink.   (b) cares and worries.   (c) alcohol abuse.

4. People who cannot stop abusing alcohol are

   (a) healthy.   (b) alcoholics.   (c) helping their bodies.

A breathing test shows if a person has had too much alcohol to drive a car safely.

The food a person eats is broken down in the digestive system. But alcohol does not pass through the digestive system. It is not broken down. Alcohol goes directly into the blood and to the brain.

As alcohol gets to brain cells, the brain works more slowly. The person may lose balance. It becomes hard to speak clearly. The person may become silly or angry. Because a person who has been drinking reacts more slowly to things, it is dangerous for that person to drive. These effects can begin soon after a person has had small amounts of alcohol. The effects last a long time, 1 hour for only ½ ounce of alcohol.

But what happens if a person drinks heavily for a long time? Alcohol destroys liver cells. When liver cells die, the liver can no longer filter wastes or help to digest foods. A person with this kind of liver disease may die.

Alcohol abuse can also lead to heart diseases. Sometimes, the heart tissues become so damaged that the heart cannot pump blood properly.

People who abuse alcohol often lose their memories. After years of heavy drinking, their hands may shake. In fact, alcohol abusers may not be able to do simple, everyday activities.

Alcohol abuse can lead to addiction. People who are addicted to alcohol are not able to make their own choices anymore. Their bodies must have alcohol. It is hard and painful to break alcohol addiction.

A. Mark with an <u>X</u> the effects of small amounts of alcohol. Mark with a ✓ the effects of abusing alcohol.

1. The brain works more slowly. _____

2. A person cannot do simple, everyday activities. _____

3. Liver cells are destroyed. _____

4. A person may lose his/her balance. _____

5. A person becomes addicted to alcohol. _____

6. A person may become silly or angry. _____

B. Answer <u>True</u> or <u>False</u>.

1. Drinking small amounts of alcohol is abusing alcohol. _____

2. Alcohol is broken down in the digestive system. _____

3. It is hard and painful to break alcohol addiction. _____

4. Alcohol can make it hard to speak clearly. _____

5. People who abuse alcohol can lose their memories. _____

6. A small amount of alcohol has no effect on a person. _____

7. Alcohol can destroy liver cells. _____

C. Fill in the missing words.

1. Alcohol goes directly into the blood, then to the _____. (brain, digestive system)

2. Alcohol can make people react _____ to the things around them. (quickly, slowly)

3. After years of drinking, a person's _____ may shake. (hands, liver)

4. As alcohol gets to the brain cells, a person may lose _____. (blood, balance)

5. Alcohol abuse can lead to _____. (lung cancer, heart diseases)

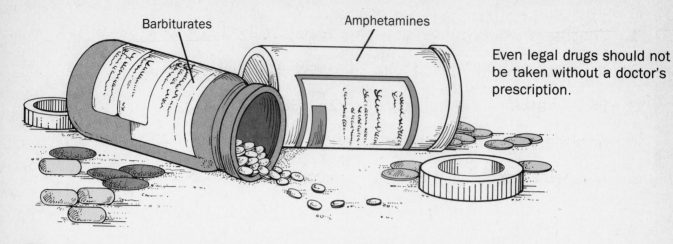

Barbiturates

Amphetamines

Even legal drugs should not be taken without a doctor's prescription.

A **drug** is a substance other than food that changes the way the body works. You have read how alcohol changes the way the body works. Alcohol is a drug. Some drugs, like alcohol, are legal. You can buy legal drugs like aspirin in stores. Other drugs are illegal. They can be bought only on the street.

Some legal drugs are **prescribed** by doctors. These drugs help sick people get well. But even these drugs can be abused.

Barbiturates are legal drugs. They slow down the nervous system. For this reason, they are known as "downers." Doctors may prescribe barbiturates for people who have trouble sleeping. But taking barbiturates when a doctor has not prescribed them is abusing them. An **overdose,** or taking too much at one time, can kill a person. Mixing barbiturates and alcohol can also lead to death.

Amphetamines are legal drugs that speed up the nervous system. For this reason, they are called "speed" or "uppers." Doctors may prescribe amphetamines for people who need to lose weight. Other people take the drug for the excited feeling it gives them. As the drug wears off, the drug user feels bad and wants more to feel better.

Barbiturates and amphetamines change the speed of the heartbeat. When these drugs are abused, they can cause **heart failure.**

A. Draw lines between the words and the descriptions that match them.

1. drug   speed up the nervous system

2. to abuse   to use something the wrong way

3. barbiturates   too much at one time

4. overdose   slow down the nervous system

5. amphetamines   changes the way the body works

B. Answer True or False.

1. A drug is food. _____

2. Alcohol is a drug. _____

3. Legal drugs can be bought in stores. _____

4. Only certain illegal drugs can be abused. _____

5. Barbiturates are legal drugs. _____

6. Barbiturates are known as "downers." _____

7. Doctors may prescribe amphetamines. _____

8. Some people take amphetamines for the excited feeling the drug gives them. _____

C. Fill in the missing words.

1. The nervous system is slowed down by _____. (barbiturates, amphetamines)

2. Using a drug the wrong way or using too much of it is _____ the drug. (prescribing, abusing)

3. Illegal drugs cannot be bought _____. (in stores, on the street)

4. Amphetamines are also called _____. (uppers, downers)

5. Drugs that doctors tell people to take are _____. (illegal, prescribed)

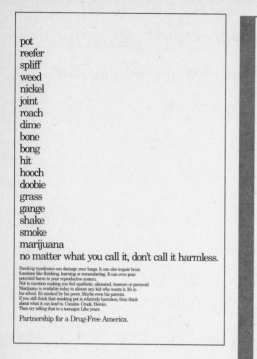

pot
reefer
spliff
weed
nickel
joint
roach
dime
bone
bong
hit
hooch
doobie
grass
gange
shake
smoke
marijuana
no matter what you call it, don't call it harmless.

Smoking marijuana can damage your lungs. It can also impair brain
functions like thinking, learning or remembering. It can even pose
potential harm to your reproductive system.
Not to mention making you feel apathetic, alienated, insecure or paranoid.
Marijuana is available today to almost any kid who wants it. It's in
his school. It's smoked by his peers. Maybe even his parents.
If you still think that smoking pot is relatively harmless, then think
about what it can lead to. Cocaine. Crack. Heroin.
Then try telling that to a teenager. Like yours.

Partnership for a Drug-Free America.

This year, 15,000 cocaine users are in for a real rush.

In 1985, 13,501 cocaine users in the U.S. were rushed to hospital emergency rooms for emergency treatment. Of those, 660 died.
That was two years ago. This year thousands more people will probably try cocaine. Cocaine is not safe. Cocaine is not recreational. In any form, cocaine is a serious health risk with deadly side effects. And it's a drug more addictive than heroin.
If you try cocaine, you may be in for more than just a high—you may be in for a real rush.
Information based on National Institute on Drug Abuse statistics.

FACE THE FACTS: DRUGS ARE A DEAD END
Partnership for a Drug-Free America.

Using illegal drugs just once can be dangerous.

Some drugs are illegal because they are dangerous. Even using some of these drugs just once is dangerous.

Marijuana is the most widely used illegal drug in the United States. It is also known as "pot" or "grass." It is usually smoked. Smoking marijuana has some of the same harmful effects as smoking tobacco. Also, smoking marijuana can affect a person's memory and learning.

Cocaine, which is also illegal, is a stronger drug than marijuana. It is usually snorted, or sniffed through the nose. Cocaine speeds up the nervous system. When cocaine is abused, it can seriously damage the inside of the nose. A form of cocaine called **crack** is more dangerous. Crack is usually smoked in a pipe. The smoke makes the heart beat fast. Using crack can also lead to heart failure. Both cocaine and crack cause people to become addicted very quickly.

Heroin, one of the strongest illegal drugs, is usually injected. It dulls the senses and gives a good feeling to the user. But a person quickly becomes addicted. For a heroin addict, only one thing matters in life—how to get the next heroin injection.

There is a special danger with heroin. It is usually mixed with other substances. Because it is bought on the street, users cannot be sure of how strong it is. They also don't know what it has been mixed with. Users can easily take too much, or an overdose, which can kill them.

A. **Answer True or False.**

1. Some drugs are illegal because they are dangerous. _____

2. Only long-term use of illegal drugs is dangerous. _____

3. Smoking marijuana does not have any of the harmful effects of smoking tobacco. _____

4. Crack is a less dangerous form of cocaine. _____

5. A person becomes addicted to heroin very fast. _____

6. Heroin users can easily take an overdose. _____

B. **Circle the letter of the correct answer.**

1. Too much of a drug at one time is called an
   (a) accident.   (b) overdose.   (c) amphetamine.

2. Using some illegal drugs just once is
   (a) legal.   (b) healthy.   (c) dangerous.

3. Getting the next injection is all that matters to an addict of
   (a) heroin.   (b) tobacco.   (c) marijuana.

4. Using crack cannot lead to
   (a) addiction.   (b) heart failure.   (c) good health.

5. A person's memory and learning can be affected by smoking
   (a) marijuana.   (b) tobacco.   (c) barbiturates.

C. **Answer the questions.**

1. Why are some drugs illegal? _____

   _____

2. Why is there a special danger in buying heroin on the street? ____

   _____

   _____

   _____

People can have fun without drugs.

What are you going to wear tomorrow? What are you going to eat for lunch? What are you going to do next Saturday?

There are always easy questions like these for you to answer. But there are more difficult questions you have to answer about your future. Are you going to make healthy choices?

Are you going to smoke? Should you go out drinking? Will you use cocaine or crack? Only you can answer these questions. Think before you answer. You must know the facts. Then decide for yourself about tobacco, alcohol, and drugs. Your health is up to you.

Answer the questions.

1. What should you do before you decide about tobacco, alcohol, and drugs? _____

   _____

2. Look at the drawing. What are some fun things people can do without drugs? _____

   _____

3. What are some fun things you like to do without drugs? _____

   _____

   _____

122

Review

Part A

Read each sentence. Write <u>True</u> if the sentence is true and <u>False</u> if it is false.

1. Smoking can have harmful effects on the body. _____

2. Drinking alcohol cannot harm the body. _____

3. Alcohol abuse can lead to addiction. _____

4. A drug is a substance other than food that changes the way the body works. _____

5. Legal drugs are never dangerous to your body. _____

6. Some drugs are illegal because they are dangerous. _____

7. Your health is up to you. _____

Part B

Write the letter for the missing word in the sentences below.

a. wine	d. overdose	g. prescribe
b. alcoholism	e. illegal	h. heroin
c. drugs	f. nicotine	i. marijuana

1. Although a doctor may _____ barbiturates, they can still be abused.

2. Taking too much of a drug at one time is an _____.

3. Alcohol abuse can lead to a serious addiction called _____.

4. One of the strongest illegal drugs is _____.

5. Substances that change the way the body works are _____.

6. It is very difficult for smokers to break _____ addiction.

7. The reason some drugs are _____ is that they are dangerous.

8. Smoking _____ has some of the harmful effects of tobacco.

Fill in the circle in front of the word or phrase that best completes the sentence. The first one is done for you.

1. Alcohol abuse can destroy
   - ● liver cells.
   - ⓑ bones.
   - ⓒ hair cells.

2. Cocaine speeds up
   - ⓐ learning.
   - ⓑ dreaming.
   - ⓒ the nervous system.

3. Using drugs the wrong way or taking too much is
   - ⓐ healthy.
   - ⓑ abuse.
   - ⓒ grown-up.

4. The addictive drug in tobacco is
   - ⓐ carbon monoxide.
   - ⓑ tar.
   - ⓒ nicotine.

5. Taking too much of a drug at one time is
   - ⓐ an overdose.
   - ⓑ safe.
   - ⓒ smoking.

6. Some chemicals in the tar in cigarette smoke can cause
   - ⓐ cancer.
   - ⓑ accidents.
   - ⓒ people to lose their balance.

7. Barbiturates, or "downers," help people
   - ⓐ wake up.
   - ⓑ sleep.
   - ⓒ run faster.

8. Alcohol goes directly to the
   - ⓐ brain.
   - ⓑ digestive system.
   - ⓒ inside of the nose.

9. People can very quickly become addicted to
   - ⓐ water.
   - ⓑ carbon monoxide.
   - ⓒ crack.

10. Tobacco smoke in the air can be
    - ⓐ healthy.
    - ⓑ harmful.
    - ⓒ clean.

Use the clues to complete the crossword puzzle. Choose words from the list.

abuse	crack	nicotine
addiction	drug	overdose
alcohol	heroin	tar
cigarette	lung	wine

Across

1. a substance in beer, wine, and whiskey
3. Smoking can lead to mouth, throat, and _____ cancer.
5. the sticky, dark substance in tobacco smoke
6. a very addictive form of cocaine
7. has tobacco in it
9. has alcohol in it
10. too much of a drug at one time

Down

1. can come from drug abuse
2. a strong, illegal drug that is usually injected
4. the addictive drug in tobacco
8. using drugs the wrong way or using too much of them
11. a substance that changes the way the body works

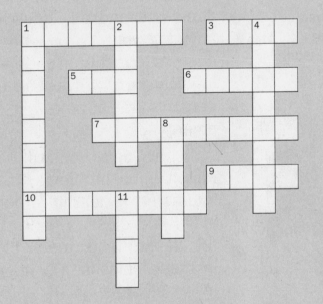

Learning First Aid

1. Call for help.

2. Tell where the injured person is. Tell what happened to the person.

3. Ask what you should do until help comes.

"Aid" means help. **First aid** means the first help you give to someone who has been in an accident, has suddenly become ill, or has been injured.

Suppose you are near someone who has been injured and needs first aid. If the injury is serious, do <u>not</u> move the person. The most important things to do are to keep calm and get medical help for the injured person. Keep a list of **emergency** phone numbers near your telephone. If you are not at home and do not have a list of emergency numbers, dial **0,** and the operator will help you.

When you call for help, be ready to tell what has happened to the injured person, anything you have done to help, and exactly where the person is. A doctor or other medical person may tell you what you can do to help the injured person. Write down the directions. Repeat the directions and ask questions about anything you do not understand. Follow the doctor's directions until an ambulance or medical help arrives. You can save a person's life by knowing what to do in an emergency.

In this unit, you will read about first aid for common problems. If you are interested in learning more, you can take a first-aid class. The Red Cross and many fire departments teach classes in first aid. In these classes, you can learn what to do in an emergency.

A. Fill in the missing words.

1. The first help you give to someone who has been in an accident is _____. (first aid, an emergency)

2. If an injury is serious, you should not _____ the person. (move, talk to)

3. The most important thing to do for an injured person is to _____. (get excited, get medical help)

4. Until medical help arrives, you should _____ the doctor's directions. (ask questions about, follow)

B. Answer True or False.

1. You should keep a list of emergency phone numbers near your telephone. _____

2. "Aid" means first. _____

3. Since you are not a doctor, a doctor will not tell you what to do to help an injured person. _____

4. You should ask questions about any doctor's directions that you do not understand. _____

C. Answer the questions.

1. What is first aid? _____

_____

_____

2. What are the most important things to do if someone near you needs first aid? _____

_____

3. Where are two places to go to take a first-aid class? _____

_____

Poisoning

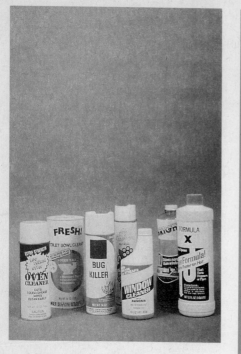

Many products found in the home have poisons in them.

Poisons are substances that are harmful if they get into your body. Many cleaners found in most homes contain poisons. Paint, gasoline, and bleach are poisons. So are products used to kill weeds and insects.

Medicines can be poisonous if taken in large amounts. For example, aspirin is safe when the directions on the label are followed. But aspirin can become a poison if it is taken in large amounts. It is important to keep medicine and poisonous products out of the reach of small children.

If someone has swallowed a poison, you must keep calm but act quickly. Call a **poison control center.** You can find this number on the first page of a telephone book, or dial **0** for help. Get the container of the poison or medicine swallowed. Tell the poison control center what kind of poison the person swallowed. Then do exactly what you are told to do.

A. Fill in the missing words.

1. Some cleaning products are _____. (drugs, poisons)

2. If you think someone has swallowed a poison, call the nearest

   _____. (friend, poison control center)

B. Answer True or False.

1. Medicines can never be poisonous. _____

2. If you call the poison control center, you should do exactly what

   you are told to do. _____

Eye Problems

Most people never have serious problems with their eyes. But small eye problems may require first aid. Some even need a doctor's care.

Suppose an eyelash or a speck of dirt gets into your eye. First wash your hands with soap and water. Then gently pull down your lower eyelid. Carefully remove the dirt with the corner of a soft, clean cloth.

If this does not work, hold your upper eyelashes. Gently pull your lid out and down. Your eye should get wet with tears. The tears may wash the object out. If they do not, gently wash your eye with water poured from a clean glass. If nothing works, call a doctor.

Getting chemicals in the eye can be dangerous. Wash the eye by pouring water into it from a clean glass. Wash the eye for 15 to 20 minutes. Then see a doctor.

Even small eye problems may need first aid.

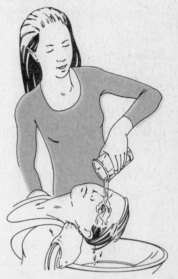

If chemicals get in your eye, pour water into the eye for 15 to 20 minutes.

A. Answer the questions.

1. If something is in your eye, why should you pull the upper lid out and down? _____

_____

2. What first aid would you use if a chemical gets in your eye? _____

_____

_____

B. Underline the correct word.

1. Sometimes the eye washes itself with (chemicals, tears).

2. Use a clean (sink, cloth) to get something out of your eye.

Fainting

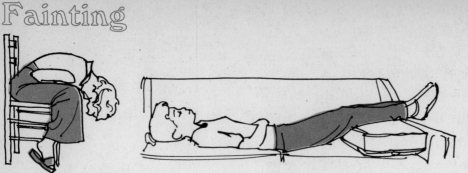

Lowering the head helps prevent fainting. If someone has already fainted, raise her legs higher than her head.

If a person's brain does not receive enough blood for a moment, the person may **faint.** A person who faints becomes unconscious. Fainting can happen suddenly, or there may be some warning signs. Before fainting, a person might become pale, dizzy, or start to sweat.

When someone shows the warning signs of fainting, try to prevent the person from falling. The person should lie down, or sit, bending the head down between the knees. Lowering the head helps send more blood to the brain. This prevents fainting. Next, help the person to breathe more easily. Loosen any tight clothing. Wet the person's face with a wet cloth.

If someone has already fainted, raise the legs higher than the head. In this position, more blood flows to the brain. The person should wake up in minutes. If it takes longer, call a doctor. A person who faints often should see a doctor.

A. Answer True or False.

1. If the brain does not get enough blood, a person may faint.

   _____

2. A person who feels dizzy should lie down. _____

B. Underline the correct word.

1. A person about to faint should (raise, lower) his or her head.

2. You should (raise, lower) the legs of a person who has fainted.

Cuts and Other Wounds

Wounds are cuts and breaks in the skin that bleed. Small wounds can be made to stop bleeding easily and quickly.

If you are cut, the bleeding itself will carry dirt out of the wound. Use a clean cotton pad to clean around the wound. If it is not cleaned, germs can get into the wound. Germs can cause an **infection.** An infection is the growth of harmful germs in the blood. If it is a small cut, the bleeding should stop soon. If it does not, press a clean cotton pad over the wound for a few minutes. When bleeding stops, **bandage** the cut.

A doctor should see wounds from animal bites. Some animals carry germs that cause disease. These germs can enter the blood of someone the animal bites. If the animal can be found, a doctor can have it tested for disease. A nail or any sharp object that punctures, or cuts into, the skin can also bring germs into the blood. A puncture wound should be seen by a doctor.

Wound	Look For	First Aid
small cut	light bleeding	press with clean cotton pad, bandage
serious cut	heavy bleeding	see a doctor
puncture	hole in skin, a little blood	wash, cover with clean bandage, call doctor

Answer True or False.

1. You can easily stop the bleeding from small wounds. _____

2. Bleeding will carry dirt into most wounds. _____

3. If a wound is not cleaned, harmful germs can get into it and cause an infection. _____

4. A puncture wound should be seen by a doctor. _____

Burns

Common Causes of Burns
first-degree burns and second-degree burns: sunburn, touching a hot object, spilling hot liquid on skin
third-degree burns: fire, spilling hot liquid or a chemical on skin

How serious a burn is depends on how deeply the skin has been burned. In a **first-degree burn,** only the top layer of skin is burned. The skin looks red and may be swollen. In a **second-degree burn,** more than one layer of skin is burned. The skin is red and swollen and may have blisters. In a **third-degree burn,** all the layers of the skin are burned. The skin may look black.

For a first-degree burn, soak the skin in cool water. Pat dry with a clean cloth. Then put a bandage over the area.

For a second-degree burn, follow the same steps for a first-degree burn. Do not break any blisters on the skin. Call a doctor right away.

For a third-degree burn, call a doctor immediately. While you wait, try to protect the person from infection. Put a clean cloth over the burn. Do not try to remove any clothing that may be stuck to the person's skin.

Underline the correct word or words.

1. First-degree burns make (every, the top) layer of skin turn red.

2. First aid (can, cannot) help a first-degree burn.

3. For first-degree burns and second-degree burns, soak the skin in (hot, cool) water.

4. For a third-degree burn, try to protect the person from (sunburn, infection).

5. Cloth or bandages used for burns should be (white, clean).

Nosebleeds

Have you ever had a nosebleed? Did your nose bleed from both nostrils? Probably not. A nosebleed is usually from one nostril.

An injury or a cold can cause a nosebleed. Playing hard or running fast can also cause a nosebleed. Sometimes a person can get a sudden nosebleed. It seems to have no cause. But most nosebleeds are not serious. They usually can be stopped quickly.

If you have a nosebleed, sit down and lean forward. Press a finger against the side of the nose that is bleeding. Hold it there firmly for 5 to 10 minutes. The nosebleed should stop. If it does not stop, hold a cold cloth against the nose for a few minutes. After the bleeding stops, do not blow your nose for several hours.

If you follow these steps and the bleeding does not stop, see a doctor. Also, anyone who gets nosebleeds often should see a doctor.

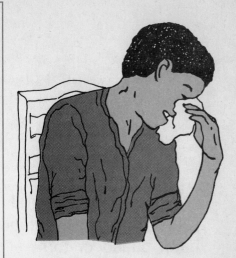

Most nosebleeds can be stopped quickly.

A. **Answer True or False.**

1. A nosebleed is never caused by an injury. _____

2. Nosebleeds are always serious. _____

3. You can stop a nosebleed by yourself. _____

B. **Answer the question.**

What are the first three steps to take to stop a nosebleed? _____

_____

_____

Sprains and Bruises

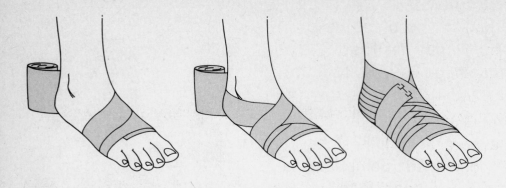

Wrap a bandage around a sprained ankle.

Have you ever **sprained** your ankle? If you have, you know it hurts. It hurts because ligaments have been pulled or torn. Ligaments are strong tissues that hold bones together.

If a sprain is in the knee or ankle, do not try to walk for at least a day. Put an ice pack on the sprain to keep the swelling down. Put a bandage around the sprained knee or ankle. When you try to walk, take it easy. If days pass and you still feel pain and the swelling has not gone down, you should go to a doctor.

Sometimes, you can fall and get bruises. Bruises are caused by bleeding under the skin. The bleeding makes the bruised skin darker. Bruises can hurt a lot. They can swell, too. Pressing a cold, wet cloth on the bruised skin should make it feel better.

Fill in the missing word or words.

1. If ligaments in your ankle are pulled or torn, you have a

   _____. (first-degree burn, sprain)

2. You can help the swelling from a sprain go down by using

   _____. (a hot cloth, an ice pack)

3. Bleeding under the skin causes a _____. (bruise, sprain)

4. Bruised skin gets darker because of _____.
   (swelling, bleeding)

Review

Part A

Fill in the missing words.

1. You should call a poison control center if someone has swallowed

   _____. (milk, a poison)

2. If ligaments are torn, a person has a _____. (nosebleed, sprain)

3. The first help you give to someone who has been injured is called

   _____. (a poison control center, first aid)

4. A person with warning signs of _____ should sit bending
   his or her head down. (a sprain, fainting)

5. Nosebleeds can usually be stopped _____.
   (only by a doctor, quickly)

6. The most important thing you should do in an emergency is

   _____. (take a first-aid class, get medical help)

Part B

Answer True or False.

1. Many cleaners found in most homes contain poisons. _____

2. For second-degree burns and third-degree burns, medical help is

   needed. _____

3. You can remove a speck of dirt from your eye with a soft, clean

   cloth. _____

4. Germs in a wound that is not cleaned can cause an infection.

   _____

5. Special first-aid courses can be taken only by doctors. _____

6. Heat slows down swelling and makes a bruise feel better. _____

Fill in the circle in front of the word or phrase that best completes the sentence. The first one is done for you.

1. In large amounts, aspirin can be
    ⓐ first aid.
    ● a poison.
    ⓒ a help.

2. Knowing what to do in an emergency can help
    ⓐ prevent sprains.
    ⓑ cause infections.
    ⓒ save lives.

3. Dirt in an eye should be washed out with
    ⓐ water.
    ⓑ soap.
    ⓒ chemicals.

4. Bleeding under the skin causes
    ⓐ nosebleeds.
    ⓑ bruises.
    ⓒ fainting.

5. All layers of skin are burned in
    ⓐ first-degree burns.
    ⓑ second-degree burns.
    ⓒ third-degree burns.

6. When the brain does not get enough blood, a person can
    ⓐ get a nosebleed.
    ⓑ faint.
    ⓒ get an infection.

7. Germs can enter the blood from
    ⓐ an animal bite.
    ⓑ a poison.
    ⓒ a sprain.

8. Help for an injured person is
    ⓐ first aid.
    ⓑ a sprain.
    ⓒ a first-aid class.

9. For a first-degree burn,
    ⓐ soak the skin in cool water.
    ⓑ break any skin blisters.
    ⓒ call a doctor immediately.

10. The legs of a person who has fainted should be
    ⓐ placed in cold water.
    ⓑ raised higher than the head.
    ⓒ bandaged.

Just for Fun

Each sentence below is about first aid. But a word is missing in each sentence. Fill in the missing words. Use the words below. When you are finished, read the circled letters from top to bottom for good advice.

ankle	clean	nose
bites	eye	poisons
bleed	faint	sprain
bruise	head	tears
burns	infections	

1. Wounds are cuts in the skin that   _ ◯ _ _ _ .

2. Use water to wash chemicals out of the   ◯ _ _ .

3. It hurts to sprain your   ◯ _ _ _ _ .

4. Bleeding under the skin is a   _ ◯ _ _ _ _ .

5. There are three degrees of   _ _ _ ◯ _ .

6. A person who sweats and becomes dizzy may   ◯ _ _ _ _ .

7. Substances that are harmful to the body are   _ ◯ _ _ _ _ .

8. Pulled or torn ligaments cause a   _ _ ◯ _ _ _ .

9. A cold cloth can stop bleeding from the   _ _ ◯ _ .

10. Dirt in the eye may be washed out by   ◯ _ _ _ _ .

11. To prevent an infection, keep a cut   _ _ _ ◯ _ .

12. A doctor should see wounds from animal   _ ◯ _ _ .

13. If you feel faint, lower your   _ _ _ ◯ .

137

GLOSSARY

abuse, page 114.
Abuse is using something too much or in the wrong way.

addictive drug, page 112.
An addictive drug is one that the body gets used to and wants all the time.

AIDS, page 100.
AIDS is a condition caused by a virus that destroys white blood cells.

air sac, page 54.
Air sacs are the ends of the tubes going into the lungs.

alcohol, page 76.
Alcohol is a drink that can slow down the nervous system.

alcoholism, page 114.
Alcoholism is a serious addiction to alcohol.

amphetamine, page 118.
Amphetamines are drugs that speed up the nervous system.

antibody, page 98.
Antibodies are chemicals made by the body that destroy germs.

artery, page 30.
Arteries are the blood vessels that carry blood away from the heart.

backbone, page 18.
The backbone is a column of vertebrae in the middle of the back.

bacteria, pages 52, 92.
Bacteria are one-celled living things. Some bacteria live in the large intestine and break down waste. Some bacteria cause disease.

balanced diet, page 44.
Eating daily from all four food groups gives a person a balanced diet.

ball-and-socket joint, page 22.
A ball-and-socket joint is a joint that can move in all directions.

bandage, page 131.
A bandage is a cloth used to cover a wound.

barbiturate, page 118.
Barbiturates are drugs that slow down the nervous system.

biology, page 4.
Biology is the study of living things.

birth canal, page 84.
The birth canal, or vagina, is the tube a baby passes through when it is born.

bladder, page 53.
The bladder is an organ that holds urine, the liquid waste from the body.

blood, page 34.
Blood is the red liquid that flows through the circulatory system.

blood pressure, page 30.
Blood pressure is the push of blood against the walls of the blood vessels.

blood vessel, page 30.
Blood vessels are the paths that blood takes through the body.

caffeine, page 76.
Caffeine is a substance that can make the nervous system too active.

calorie, page 46.
The energy in food is measured in calories.

cancer, page 104.
Cancer is a disorder in which body cells grow and multiply much faster than normal.

capillary, page 30.
Capillaries are the tiny blood vessels that bring food and oxygen to body cells.

carbohydrate, page 40.
Carbohydrates are nutrients that are used to produce energy.

carbon monoxide, page 112.
Carbon monoxide is a poisonous gas given off by burning tobacco and by cars.

cartilage, page 20.
Cartilage is the part of the skeleton that is softer than bone.

cells, page 6.
Cells are the smallest parts of all living things.

central nervous system, page 64.
The central nervous system directs all actions of the body. It is made up of the brain and the spinal cord.

cereals and breads, page 44.
Cereals and breads are foods in one of the four basic food groups.

chamber, page 32.
The heart is divided into four parts called chambers.

chicken pox, page 94.
Chicken pox is a disease that is caused by a virus.

cholesterol, page 102.
Cholesterol is a kind of fat that can block arteries.

chromosome, page 88.
Chromosomes are parts of cells that carry the information needed to grow and develop.

circulatory system, page 28.
The circulatory system controls the movement of blood through the body. It is made up of the heart, the blood, and the blood vessels.

cocaine, page 120.
Cocaine is an illegal drug that speeds up the nervous system.

cold, page 94.
A cold is a disease that is caused by a virus.

crack, page 120.
Crack is a dangerous form of the illegal drug cocaine.

dairy, page 44.
Dairy foods make up one of the four basic food groups. Milk and milk products are dairy foods.

diaphragm, page 54.
The diaphragm is a large muscle that controls the lungs and breathing.

digestion, page 48.
Digestion is the breaking down of food into nutrients.

digestive system, page 48.
The digestive system breaks down food into nutrients. It is made up of the mouth, the stomach, the small intestine, and the large intestine.

disease, page 92.
A disease is an illness where some part of the body does not work properly.

disorder, page 102.
Disorders are diseases that last a long time or that get worse in time.

drug, page 118.
A drug is a substance other than food that changes the way the body works.

ear canal, page 68.
The ear canal is the tube that leads from the outer ear to the inside of the ear.

eardrum, page 68.
The eardrum is a thin skin that covers the end of the ear canal.

egg cell, page 84.
Egg cells are the female reproductive cells stored in ovaries. When a sperm cell joins with an egg cell, fertilization takes place.

emergency, page 126.
An emergency is a sudden need for help.

excretory system, page 52.
The excretory system is the system that removes waste from the body.

faint, page 130.
When a person faints, he or she becomes unconscious.

fat cell, page 8.
Fat cells are body cells that store fat.

fat, page 40.
Fats are nutrients that give the body energy.

fertilization, page 82.
Fertilization takes place when a sperm cell from a male joins with an egg cell from a female.

fetus, page 84.
A fetus is a fertilized egg that grows into a baby.

first aid, page 126.
First aid is the first help you give to someone who is hurt or ill.

first-degree burn, page 132.
In a first-degree burn, only the top layer of skin is burned.

flu, page 94.
The flu is a disease that is caused by a virus.

food group, page 44.
Foods are divided into four basic food groups. These groups give a person all the nutrients he or she needs.

gallbladder, page 50.
The gallbladder is an organ that helps in the digestion of fats.

gene, page 88.
Genes are the parts of chromosomes that determine traits.

germ, page 98.
Germs are bacteria or viruses that can cause disease.

gland, page 80.
Glands are organs that make special chemicals, or hormones, in the body.

heart, page 32.
The heart is the organ that pumps blood through the body.

heart attack, page 102.
A heart attack occurs when less blood reaches the heart. When this happens, parts of the heart may die.

heart disease, page 102.
Heart diseases are disorders that affect the heart or the blood vessels.

heart failure, page 118.
Heart failure takes place when the heart cannot work in the normal way.

heart muscle, page 26.
Heart muscle makes the heart beat and pumps blood to all parts of the body.

heredity, page 88.
Heredity is the passing on of traits from parents to children.

heroin, page 120.
Heroin is one of the strongest illegal drugs.

hinge joint, page 22.
A hinge joint is a joint that can bend back and forth in one direction.

hormone, page 80.
Hormones are special chemicals made by the glands of the body.

identical twin, page 88.
Identical twins are people with exactly the same traits.

infection, page 131.
An infection is the growth of harmful germs in the blood.

injection, page 99.
An injection is a way of getting liquid into the body through a needle.

involuntary muscle, page 26.
Involuntary muscles are those that a person does not control.

iris, page 66.
The iris is the colored part of the eye.

iron, page 34.
Iron is a mineral. Red blood cells need iron to carry oxygen.

joint, page 22.
Joints are places where two bones come together.

kidney, page 53.
The kidneys are the main organs of the excretory system. They filter out water, salts, and harmful chemicals.

large intestine, page 48.
The large intestine is an organ of the digestive system. Waste passes out of the body through the large intestine.

larynx, page 74.
The larynx, or voice box, contains the vocal cords.

lens, page 66.
The lens is the part of the eye that can focus light.

ligament, page 22.
Ligaments are strong, threadlike tissues that hold bones together.

liver, page 50.
The liver is an organ that helps in digestion of fats.

lungs, page 54.
The lungs are the main organs of the respiratory system.

mammal, page 86.
Mammals belong to a group of animals that have glands that make milk.

marijuana, page 120.
Marijuana is an illegal drug that is usually smoked. It can affect a person's memory and learning.

marrow, page 20.
Marrow is the soft material inside a bone. Red blood cells are made in the marrow.

measles, page 94.
Measles is a disease that is caused by a virus.

meat, page 44.
Meat is one of the four basic food groups.

membrane, page 8.
The membrane is the outer part of a cell.

menstrual cycle, page 84.
The menstrual cycle takes place about once a month in females. In part of the cycle, blood from the tissue of the uterus flows out of the body.

microscope, page 6.
A microscope is a tool that lets you see objects that are too small to see with your eyes alone.

mineral, page 42.
Minerals are nutrients that help other nutrients do their jobs.

motor nerve, page 62.
Motor nerves are nerves that cause muscles to move.

mouth, page 48.
The mouth is a part of the digestive system. Food enters the body through the mouth.

mucus, page 96.
Mucus is a sticky liquid made in the tissues that line the nose and throat.

mumps, page 94.
Mumps is a disease that is caused by a virus.

muscular system, page 24.
The muscular system is made up of all the muscles of the body.

navel, page 86.
The navel is the place where the umbilical cord was attached to the developing baby.

nerve cell, page 8.
Nerve cells are body cells that carry messages through the body.

nerve, page 62.
Nerves are made up of bundles of cells called neurons.

nervous system, page 62.
The nervous system is the system that gets information from other parts of the body and from the environment. Then it tells the body what to do.

neuron, page 62.
A neuron is a cell in the nervous system. Messages move from one neuron to another.

nicotine, page 112.
Nicotine is an addictive drug that is inhaled when tobacco is smoked.

nucleus, page 8.
The nucleus is the part of the cell that gives instructions to the cell.

nutrient, page 40.
Nutrients are the parts of food the body can use.

optic nerve, page 66.
The optic nerve is the part of the eye that sends pictures to the brain.

organ, page 11.
An organ is a group of different tissues working together to do a job.

outer ear, page 68.
The outer ear is the part of the ear that you can see. It catches sound vibrations from the air.

ovary, page 80.
The ovaries are the female sex organs.

overdose, page 118.
An overdose is taking too much of a drug at one time.

pancreas, page 50.
The pancreas is an organ that helps in the digestion of fats, proteins, and starches.

penis, page 82.
The penis is an organ of the male reproductive system.

period, page 84.
A period is the time when blood from the uterus flows out of a female's body.

pituitary gland, page 80.
The pituitary gland makes a hormone that is carried to the bones.

pivot joint, page 22.
A pivot joint is a joint that can move around and back.

placenta, page 86.
The placenta is a tissue between the uterus and a developing fetus. Food and wastes pass through the placenta.

plasma, page 34.
Plasma is the liquid part of blood.

pneumonia, page 92.
Pneumonia is a serious infection of the lungs that is caused by bacteria.

poison control center, page 128.
A poison control center will tell you what to do for a person who has swallowed a poison.

poison, page 128.
Poisons are subtances that are harmful if they get into your body.

pregnant, page 86.
A female is pregnant when a fertilized egg starts to grow in her body.

prescribed, page 118.
A drug that is prescribed is ordered for a person by a doctor.

protein, page 40.
Proteins are nutrients the body uses to grow and repair tissue.

protoplasm, page 8.
Protoplasm is the clear jelly inside a cell.

puberty, page 80.
Puberty is the stage between childhood and adulthood.

pupil, page 66.
The pupil is the dark opening at the center of the eye.

pus, page 97.
Pus is made of dead bacteria and white blood cells.

radiation, page 104.
Radiation is a kind of energy that can destroy cancer cells.

rectum, page 52.
The rectum is the last part of the large intestine. Muscles in the rectum push solid waste out of the body.

red blood cell, page 34.
Red blood cells are part of the blood. They carry food and oxygen to body cells.

reflex, page 64.
A reflex is an action you do not have to think about. Blinking, sneezing, and coughing are reflexes.

reproduce, page 86.
To reproduce means to make more.

reproductive system, page 82.
The reproductive system is the system in which sperm cells or egg cells are made.

respiratory system, page 54.
The respiratory system is the system that brings oxygen into the body.

rib cage, page 18.
The rib cage is a group of bones that protects the heart and lungs.

saliva, page 48.
Saliva is a liquid found in the mouth. It mixes with food and changes the starch in food to sugar.

scrotum, page 82.
The scrotum is a sac of skin that holds the testes in males.

second-degree burn, page 132.
In a second-degree burn, more than one layer of skin is burned.

semen, page 82.
Semen is a mixture of a fluid and sperm cells.

sensory nerve, page 62.
Sensory nerves are nerves that get information from sense organs.

sex hormone, page 80.
Sex hormones are chemicals that control the development of male and female characteristics.

skeletal muscle, page 24.
Skeletal muscles are the muscles that move the bones of the skeleton.

skeletal system, page 16.
The skeletal system is made up of all the bones in the body.

skeleton, page 16.
A skeleton is the framework of bones that supports the body.

skin cell, page 8.
Skin cells are body cells that protect the parts of the body that they cover.

skull, page 18.
The skull is a group of bones that protects the eyes and the brain.

small intestine, page 48.
The small intestine is an organ of the digestive system. Nutrients pass through its walls into blood vessels.

smooth muscle, page 26.
Smooth muscles are found in the blood vessels, the stomach, and the large intestine.

sperm, page 82.
Sperm are the male reproductive cells made in the testes. When a sperm cell joins with an egg cell, fertilization takes place.

spinal cord, page 18.
The spinal cord connects the brain with other parts of the body. It is part of the nervous system.

sprained, page 134.
A body part is sprained when its ligaments have been pulled or torn.

stomach, page 48.
The stomach is an organ of the digestive system. In the stomach, food begins to break down.

stroke, page 102.
In a stroke, a blood vessel breaks and blood does not get to the brain.

system, page 12.
A system is a group of organs doing the same job.

tar, page 112.
Tar is a dark, sticky mixture of chemicals produced when tobacco burns.

taste bud, page 70.
Taste buds are the ends of sensory nerves on the tongue.

tendon, page 24.
Tendons are tissues that connect muscle to bones.

testes, page 80.
The testes are the male sex organs.

third-degree burn, page 132.
In a third-degree burn, all the layers of the skin are burned.

thyroid gland, page 80.
The thyroid gland makes a hormone that controls how fast a person changes food into energy.

tissue, page 10.
A tissue is a group of cells doing the same job.

tobacco, page 110.
Tobacco is a substance that is smoked in cigarettes, chewed, or inhaled as snuff.

toxin, page 92.
Toxins are the poisons made by the bacteria that cause disease.

trait, page 88.
Traits are features like hair color and height.

tumor, page 104.
A tumor is a mass of cancer cells.

umbilical cord, page 86.
The umbilical cord is a tissue that attaches the fetus to the placenta.

urethra, page 82.
The urethra is a tube that leads semen out of a male's body.

urine, page 53.
Urine is the liquid waste removed from the body by the excretory system.

uterus, page 84.
The uterus is an organ in the female body where a baby can grow and develop.

vaccine, page 99.
Vaccines are shots made up of bacteria or virus particles that are dead or weak.

vagina, page 84.
The vagina, or birth canal, is a passageway that leads out of a female's body.

valve, page 32.
A valve is a flap of tissue in the heart. It lets blood flow in only one direction.

vegetables and fruit, page 44.
Vegetables and fruit are foods in one of the four basic food groups.

vein, page 30.
Veins are blood vessels that bring blood back to the heart.

vertebra, page 18.
A vertebra is one of the small bones of the backbone.

vibration, page 68.
A vibration is the motion of the air that results in sound.

virus, page 94.
Viruses are tiny particles that cause disease.

vitamin, page 42.
Vitamins are nutrients that help other nutrients do their jobs.

vocal cord, page 74.
The vocal cords are folds of skin that vibrate when air passes over them.

voluntary muscle, page 26.
Voluntary muscles are muscles that move because the brain directs them to move.

white blood cell, page 34.
White blood cells are part of the blood. They help the body fight germs that cause disease.

whooping cough, page 92.
Whooping cough is a disease of the respiratory system. It is caused by bacteria.

windpipe, page 54.
The windpipe is a tube in the throat that brings air to the lungs.

wound, page 131.
Wounds are cuts and breaks in the skin that bleed.

Staff Credits

Executive Editor: Elizabeth Strauss

Supervising Editor: Kathleen Fitzgibbon

Project Editor: Susan Miller

Design Coordinator: Cynthia Ellis

Product Development

Contemporary Perspectives, Inc.

Illustrations

Accurate Art, Inc. - **94, 96, 98, 102**

Alex Bloch - **6, 8, 10, 11**

Ebet Dudley - **50, 56, 80, 82T, 84, 86**

Erika Kors - **16T, 18, 22T, 24, 30B, 32, 62T, 64, 70, 72**

Art Kretzschmar - **126, 129, 134**

Laurie O'Keefe - **114, 116, 118**

All Other Illustrations

Joe Nerlinger and Lewis Calver

Photographs

Cover   Steve Allen/Peter Arnold

Geers Gross Advertising/Partnership For a Drug-Free America—**120T**

Grant Heilman—**4B**

Michal Heron—**4T, 58, 68, 88, 128**

Manfred Kage/Peter Arnold—**34T, B, 82, 92**

David Madison—**36**

McCann-Erickson Detroit/Partnership For a Drug-Free America—**120B**

Tom McHugh/Photo Researchers, Inc.—**12**

NYC Dept. of Health—**99**

Barry Runk From Grant Heilman—**66**

Victoria Beller Smith—**40, 76**